CHRISTMAS JOKES for FUNNY BLOKES

Also published by Michael O'Mara Books

Christmas Jokes for Grumpy Blokes

All I Got for Christmas Was This Lousy Joke Book

CHRISTMAS JOKES for FUNNY BLOKES

MIKE HASKINS

Illustrated by Rob Murray

Michael O'Mara Books Limited

First published in Great Britain in 2022 by
Michael O'Mara Books Limited
9 Lion Yard
Tremadoc Road
London SW4 7NQ

A CIP catalogue record for this book is available from the
British Library.

Papers used by Michael O'Mara Books Limited are natural,
recyclable products made from wood grown in sustainable
forests. The manufacturing processes conform to the
environmental regulations of the country of origin.

ISBN: 978-1-78929-469-9 in paperback print format
ISBN: 978-1-78929-470-5 in ebook format

1 2 3 4 5 6 7 8 9 10

Cover design by Natasha Le Coultre
Designed and typeset by Design23
Printed and bound by CPI Group (UK) Ltd, Croydon, CR0 4YY
www.mombooks.com

CONTENTS

INTRODUCTION

Christmas, they say, comes but once a year. And these days it usually all begins sometime in early September. It is of course the happiest, most joyful, wonderful time of the year. Or at least it is if you are (a) under twelve years old and lucky enough to get some lovely presents or (b) permanently sozzled. For the rest of us, however, it can be the most stressful time, immediately preceded by the most exhausting, exasperating and expensive time.

But then again it is Christmas. So you really mustn't complain!

Over the years many different traditions have grown up around Christmas, and they all have to be followed whether we like them or not to ensure our enjoyment of the festive season. These days the most popular Christmas traditions include: drinking too much; eating too much; spending way too much; arguing with your partner; having to hear Christmas hit songs that you'd rather never ever hear again played on a constant loop every time you enter any retail outlet; eating and drinking yet again; being visited by relatives you'd rather not see; eating and drinking yet more; falling asleep; watching TV; complaining about what's on TV; and getting excited when the first advert for next year's summer holidays comes on.

In reality Christmas is, of course, a sacred and important festival in the Christian calendar that should inspire us to live a better, purer life, and to shun all worldly and materialistic things. It is only right, therefore, that the best bit of Christmas is being given lots of exciting, expensive presents.

At least this is the best bit if you are that pre-teenage child. Christmas is the day when you will come into possession of gargantuan amounts of toys, sweets and tat. At this age this is exactly what you want, so it doesn't matter how much rubbish you are given, you will still think Christmas is utterly brilliant. But as an adult ... no one will have a clue what to buy you. It becomes the day when people give you mad socks, underwear with slogans, David Beckham deodorant or, if you're particularly lucky, a scented candle. Now you will spend every New Year flogging these unwanted gifts on eBay, exchanging them with others, or traipsing round the shops to try to return or swap them – finding out exactly how little they cost!

Another really popular Christmas tradition is parents repeatedly lying to their children in the most extraordinary and shameless manner. Why adults choose to do this is a little unclear but, for some reason, they seem determined to trick their children into thinking that they are not responsible for the presents they have just given them. No, they all arrive thanks to a mysterious elderly man in a red suit who broke into the house during the night.

On every other day of the year except Christmas, parents spend their time trying to secure their property against intruders and telling their children that they must never talk to, or accept gifts from, strangers. At Christmas, however, all this goes out the window and the rotund man in red is allowed to illegally enter the house and wander in and out of everyone's bedroom as they sleep. And despite this happening year after year, the matter is never referred to the police.

But this isn't even the most bizarre of our accepted Christmas traditions. Another of the most common (and also most insane) festive customs involves placing a tree in the corner of the living room. In normal circumstances the only time a tree is likely to be found inside someone's home is if there has been a recent storm which has caused it to come crashing through the roof.

The first Christmas tree we know about was put up in the town of Freiburg in the Black Forest in 1419. And the joke was on them because they then had to wait over 400 years for electricity to be invented so they could plug in their lights. These days millions of trees are grown every year just so they can be cut down and sold for Christmas. Then, once the holiday is over, people take the trees down, toss them in the back of their cars and drive around the neighbourhood for hours trying to find if there is anywhere they can dispose of a now dead tree, before finally giving up and dumping it in a local beauty spot, a supermarket car park or an unsuspecting neighbour's garden. They then drive back home to spend all of January trying to vacuum up the pine needles from their carpet.

They will never be entirely successful in doing this, however, and solitary pine needles will be found lodged in socks or bare feet right through the year. Whenever this happens the entire family will be gathered to gaze in wonder upon the lone pine needle and to spend several minutes discussing its discovery. At some point at least one particularly bright member of the family will proclaim, 'It must have come from the tree we had at Christmas.' There are others, however, who realize that this sort of behaviour is bizarre. They purchase artificial effigies of trees and put these up in their living rooms instead.

While putting up a tree in your living room is bizarre behaviour, another Christmas tradition has been gaining in popularity in recent years. People now spend enormous amounts of money in decorating the outside of their houses with lights and illuminated Christmas-themed ornaments. At the first Christmas, the wise men were guided to Bethlehem by a star. These days people require the power generated by a star just to work the lights they have draped all over their house.

This represents an extraordinary level of effort and expense especially considering that the people who have put up the lights then spend the rest of Christmas sitting *inside* their houses, completely unable to see what they've just created. And they have to be inside – it's the middle of December and far too cold to be out. And so they spend Christmas sitting inside their home staring at the sad-looking tree they propped up in the corner of their living room. In fact the main pleasure families derive from these illuminations comes from watching dad climb up on the roof to put up all his hundreds of Christmas lights. Back down in the garden the rest of the family are able to look on in wonder, while placing bets on whether dad or Santa will come down the chimney first.

Food, drink, presents that nobody wants except the kids, a dying tree in the corner of the lounge and massive amounts of lights all over the house that no one can see. These are the great traditions of the modern Christmas, so it will probably come as a great surprise to many that the festival originally had something to do with a story in an obscure book called the Bible.

The 25th of December is in fact the day when we celebrate the birth of Jesus. These days, however, it's becoming increasingly difficult to celebrate Jesus's birthday because, after over 2,000 years, it's very hard to get him a present that he hasn't already been given.

Jesus was born in the town of Bethlehem where his mother Mary gave birth to him in a manger and not, as many people have come to believe in recent times, a branch of Pret a Manger. Mary and her husband, Joseph, had been forced to travel to Bethlehem to take part in a census. This means that in theory it should now be possible to find their details if you look them up on Ancestry.com. In Bethlehem Mary and Joseph found no room at the inn because not only was everyone in town for a census, it was also Christmas. Why Mary and Joseph – and so many others – had been told to go to Bethlehem to take part in a census remains unclear as the organizers must surely have known that the place was famous for being a 'little town' and therefore entirely unsuitable for such large gatherings.

Finding no room at the inn, Mary and Joseph found accommodation in a stable, although the listing on Airbnb probably described it as a quaint, alternative, rural-themed holiday retreat. Mary promptly gave birth to Jesus, worryingly close to an ox and ass, only to find a bunch of shepherds and wise men had turned up to watch. All of this would probably be frowned upon in a maternity unit today.

So, if you want to celebrate Christmas in a genuinely traditional and religious manner, clearly it's out with the trees and lighting, the booze and the turkey. Instead, you need to spend the holiday doing a census, befriending shepherds and bedding yourself down for the night with a few farm animals.

But whatever you do, have fun!

Happy Christmas!

PREPARATIONS FOR THE BIG DAY

The local council decide they want to put up some Christmas lights and decorations all over town, but they think this will be a costly job. They decide to put the work out to tender and receive bids from three different contractors. The town clerk calls each of the three contractors in for an interview.

The first contractor gives his tender for the work of £3,000 and explains to the town clerk how it breaks down: 'It's £1,000 for me, £1,000 for all the lights and £1,000 for my men to put them up.'

The town clerk thanks him, wishes him Happy Christmas and summons in the next contractor.

'My bid for the job is £6,000,' says the next man. 'That breaks down as follows: £2,000 for me £2,000 for all the lights and £2,000 for my men to put them up.'

The town clerk thanks him, wishes him Happy Christmas and asks the final contractor to come in.

The final contractor's estimate for the job turns out to be £9,000.

'Oh, my goodness,' says the clerk. 'That sounds rather expensive. How can you justify that price?'

'Well,' says the third contractor, 'let me explain. It's £3,000 for me, £3,000 for you and then we get the first guy to do the job!'

A little girl says to her mother, 'Mummy! How soon is Christmas?'

'Not long,' replies her mum. 'Why do you ask?'

'I was just wondering if it was near enough for me to start being good,' says the little girl.

Each Christmas these days people decorate the outsides of their houses with so many lights, you don't know if they're celebrating the birth of Jesus or the guy who invented the light bulb.

A man is looking through his diary and tells his friend, 'Oh look. We're quite lucky this year because Christmas falls on Christmas Day.'

'Great!' says his friend. 'That means we should get the day off.'

A man walks into a hardware shop and says, 'I'd like to buy a string of Christmas lights, please.'

'OK,' says the shop owner. 'How long do you want them?'

'Well,' says the man. 'Really I was hoping I could keep them.'

'I wanted our street to have the prettiest decorations in the neighbourhood, so I strung lit coloured balls from house to house, all the way down the block. I did all the electrical wiring myself. If you'd like further information, just drive down Moorpark Street in North Hollywood. We're the third pile of ashes from the corner.'

BOB HOPE

A primary school teacher is getting her class ready for Christmas.

She asks the children to name their favourite carols, and one little boy puts his hand up and says he likes the one about baby Jesus going to the toilet.

'I don't know that one,' says the teacher. 'Which one do you mean?'

'You know,' says the little boy, 'the one that goes "A Wee in a Manger"...'

Because it's Christmas Noddy Holder is going back out on tour with Slade performing their festive hit 'Merry Xmas Everybody'. He goes to a vintage clothing shop to get himself kitted out in his trademark 1970s outfit. At the counter he asks for a pair of tartan loon pants, a pair of platform boots and a top hat covered in mirrors.

'I'll just fetch all those for you, Mr Holder,' says the assistant. 'And what about a kipper tie to go with them?'

'Oh, ta, mate!' says Noddy. 'I'll have milk and two sugars in mine!'

It's almost Christmas, so a man decides to go to church and make his confession as he hasn't been for many years.

He walks in to the confessional and is surprised to find inside a fully equipped bar with Guinness on tap, bottles of whisky and a range of cigars. He sees the priest and kneels down and begins to pray.

'Father, forgive me,' he says. 'It's been a long time since my last confession. And I have to say the confessional is so much more inviting than I remember it being before.'

'My son,' says the priest, 'it clearly has been a very long time since your last confession because you've come in to the wrong bit. This is my side.'

A little Jewish boy is watching his neighbours across the road put up their Christmas tree in the their living room and cover it in lights.

He turns and asks his father, 'Dad, why can't we be like them? Why can't we have a Hanukkah tree?'

'Sorry, son. That's not possible,' says his dad. 'Last time we had to deal with a lighted bush we ended up having to spend forty years in the desert.'

A woman is checking her diary. 'Hey!' she says to her husband. 'Did you know that Christmas Day falls on a Friday this year?'

'Oh no!' says her husband. 'Let's hope it's not going to be on the 13th!'

They should change the date of Christmas. Every year it seems to come round at just the time when the shops are really busy.

Stan looks out of his window on 27 December.

'Will you look at that!' he says. 'Three hundred and sixty-four days until Christmas and people have already got their lights up!'

YOU KNOW YOU'VE BOUGHT A RUBBISH CHRISTMAS TREE WHEN ...

You discover the needles come in a separate box.

A shower of needles falls off it if your dog so much as shakes in the next room.

It is so small you begin to suspect it may just be a car air freshener.

Despite assurances from the salesman that it is a real tree, the branches come separately and have to be attached to the trunk.

It was purchased second hand and advertised as having only one previous owner – although that was several years ago.

It comprises a pot, a pine cone and a watering can, together with a label saying 'Some self-assembly necessary'.

It comprises one single branch and a trunk but it's difficult to tell which is which.

It is two feet tall but twenty feet wide.

If you didn't know any better, you'd swear it looked like a broom handle with a lot of coat hangers.

It comprises a real trunk and artificial branches – or possibly vice versa.

It is perfectly shaped with big branches at one end and progressively smaller branches down the trunk – but unfortunately the big branches are at the top.

If you try attaching the lightest glass bauble you possess, it will snap the branch.

THE TRUE SPIRIT OF
THE FESTIVE SEASON

On Christmas Eve, Arthur pops over to see an elderly neighbour.

Eventually the old lady comes hobbling along to open the door and Arthur says, 'Hello! I'm Arthur. Me and my wife and kids live just across the street, and we were wondering if you were going to be spending Christmas all on your own this year.'

'Yes. I'm afraid I will be,' says the old lady sadly.

'Oh dear. That's a terrible shame,' says Arthur. 'In that case I wondered if we could borrow a few chairs from you as we've got the whole family coming over?'

A man is stopped in the street by a charity worker.

'As it's coming up to Christmas,' says the charity worker, 'have you ever thought about doing some voluntary work?'

'Good heavens! No!' says the man. 'I wouldn't do that if you paid me!'

A teacher asks her class to name phrases they think sum up the true meaning of Christmas.

One child puts his hand up and says, 'Peace on Earth'.

Another child puts her hand up and suggests, 'Goodwill to Men'.

A third child then sticks his hand up and says, 'Batteries not included'!

'Once again, we come to the Holiday Season, a deeply religious time that each of us observes, in his own way, by going to the mall of his choice.'

DAVE BARRY

Dad is trying to teach his daughter the true meaning of Christmas and that it's not all about getting expensive presents. He tells her that she should be pleased with whatever she gets because when Jesus was born he only received three gifts. Then he takes her to church on Christmas Day and they hear the story of the three wise men arriving to see the baby Jesus.

Afterwards he asks his daughter what she thought Jesus might ask Father Christmas.

'I think,' says the little girl, 'he would ask how come I only got three things and not one of them was a toy?'

The world's most popular Christmas books:
Christmas Kisses by Miss L Toe

Popular Christmas Plants by Holly Bush

Favourite Christmas Songs by Carol Singer

More Favourite Christmas Songs by Emma
Dreaming, Arthur White, Chris Muss

Cooking at Christmas by Ross Turkey,
Min Spies and Brandy Butter

The definition of Christmas

The time of year when we give away lots
of things we'd really like to have and
receive lots of things we don't really
want in return.

A primary school teacher asks her class of
children to tell her what they are most thankful
about at Christmas time.

One little girl puts her hand up and says, 'I
am thankful that I am not a turkey.'

A student is on his way home from college for Christmas when a tramp stops him and asks if he has any spare change.

'Why should I give you any money?' asks the student. 'You'll only go and spend it all on drink and drugs.'

'Yeah!' says the tramp. 'So, in other words, exactly the same as *you're* going to do with it!'

In the run-up to the holiday season the Prime Minister gets a call from a TV station who ask him what he'd like for Christmas.

'Well, as you well know,' says the Prime Minister, 'in my position I can't possibly accept gifts from anyone.'

The TV people however are persistent and in the end, to shut them up, the Prime Minister says, 'OK, if you insist, I would just like a small box of lovely chocolates, please.'

A few days later, the Prime Minister is watching the television when the newsreader comes on and says:

'Earlier this month we asked a series of world

leaders what they would like for Christmas. The French President said he'd like to see peace between all warring nations, the German Chancellor said he'd like to see the starving people of the world fed and the British Prime Minister said he'd like a small box of chocolates.'

Three men are talking about their children.

The first says, 'Our son was born on St George's Day, so obviously we decided to call him George.'

'I can't believe it,' says the second. 'That's exactly the same as happened with us. We named our son David because he was born on St David's Day.'

'That's incredible!' says the third. 'That's exactly the same as happened with us and our daughter Christmas Eve.'

'The TV news people keep saying this could be the greatest Christmas we ever had. I kind of thought the first one was.'

MILTON BERLE

In the run-up to the festive season the local priest goes in to a school to give the class an RE lesson on the true meaning of the festive season and to tell the children how they must be good if they want to have a nice Christmas.

'Because,' says the priest to the class of little ones, 'you all know where all the bad little boys and girls end up going don't you?'

'Yes, we do, father,' says one of the children. 'It's behind the bike sheds!'

'My husband's idea of getting the Christmas spirit is to become Scrooge.'

MELANIE WHITE

Christmas is known as a magical time
of year for a good reason. It's the time
you can watch all your money
magically disappear.

Two grumpy old men are in the pub moaning about Christmas.

'All year long I work my fingers to the bone,' says one of the men, 'just to buy presents for my kids. But then what happens every time on Christmas morning? That fat so-and-so with the beard gets all the credit instead of me!'

'Well,' says his friend, 'you shouldn't have married her then, should you?'

Life is a bit like being one of the reindeer pulling Santa's sleigh: if you're not at the front of the pack your view rarely changes.

It's Christmas Day and a rich man looks out of his big house only to see a poor tramp down on his hands and knees on his front lawn.

The rich man opens his window and calls out: 'Oi! What do you think you're doing?'

'Sorry, sir,' says the tramp. 'But I've not eaten in weeks so I was having a nibble of the grass in your front garden.'

'This is terrible! And at Christmas as well!' says the rich man. 'Just wait there till I come out to you!'

The tramp waits until the rich man has unlocked his massive great door and walks out, takes him by the hand and leads him round the side of the house.

'Please come this way,' says the rich man. 'The grass is much longer in the back garden.'

'Adults can take a simple holiday for children and screw it up. What began as a presentation of simple gifts to delight and surprise children around the Christmas tree has culminated in a woman unwrapping six shrimp forks from her dog, who drew her name.'

ERMA BOMBECK

A man is driving through the city one day in the middle of December when he notices a little boy sitting at the side of the road crying his eyes out. The man decides he has to go and check what's the matter, so he parks his car and goes over to ask the little boy if he is all right. The boy holds up a £50 note.

'Look at this!' he says sobbing. 'I used to have two £50 notes like this. And that was all the money that my mummy had saved up through the whole year for Christmas. She gave both of the notes to me and told me to go out and use them to do all our Christmas shopping but then a horrible man came up and stole one of the £50 notes and ran away with it.'

'That's terrible,' says the man. 'Why didn't anyone passing by do anything to help you?'

'They wouldn't do anything like that round here,' says the boy. 'They all just walk past no matter what happens.'

'Oh dear,' says the man. 'Well, all I can say is that really you should have learned your lesson by now.'

And with that he grabbed the other £50 note and dashed back to his car.

A family are preparing for Christmas but they are worried about their elderly neighbour across the street. In the spirit of the season, the mum thinks she'd better send her young son across to check on her and tells him: 'Pop across the road and go and see how old Mrs Smith is for me?'

A few minutes later the boy comes back and his mum asks: 'Is Mrs Smith all right?'

'Yes,' says the boy, 'but you've really annoyed her now.'

'What do you mean?' says mum. 'How have I annoyed her?'

'She says it's none of your business how old she is,' says the boy.

Always remember – good friends are just like snowballs. They will go away if you pee on them.

SHOP UNTIL THE PINE NEEDLES DROP

Every year, Christmas becomes less like Jesus's birthday and more like a clearance sale.

A couple are going round the shopping centre.

The woman says, 'Look at the lovely twinkling Christmas lights. And look at all the delicious Christmas food laid out. And look at all those exciting toys and presents for the children. And look at the incredible models of Father Christmas and his reindeer. And look at those snowmen. And all the classic Christmas songs and carols playing constantly everywhere you go.'

'Yes,' says her husband. 'How I love August!'

It's late on Christmas Eve and Bob and Tanya are driving around the city centre trying to find a parking space to do their Christmas shopping before everything closes.

In the end, in complete desperation, Bob prays to heaven: 'Oh God, please let us find a parking space. If you do this for us we will never doubt you again and we will devote our entire lives to you from this day forward, give up drinking and sex and ...'

'Actually, God,' says Tanya, digging Bob sharply in the ribs and pointing out a space that has just come free, 'No need to worry after all! We've just found one!'

It's December and a man goes to his doctor and says, 'Doctor, you've got to help me. I'm a terrible kleptomaniac and every time I walk into a shop I just start stealing as much stuff as I can.'

'OK,' says the doctor. 'Here are some pills that might help. But in case you find they don't work, can I give you a list of all the things my wife and children have asked for for Christmas?'

Shirley tells her granddad that Amazon is the best place to do all your Christmas shopping these days. A few days later she gets a call from Brazil asking what she would like.

Martin manages to get himself arrested while he's doing his Christmas shopping. It turns out that when the woman on the checkout told him, 'Strip down, facing me' she was actually referring to his credit card.

One year, Brian decided to do his Christmas shopping early in order to avoid the rush, but despite doing it a whole twelve months early he found the shops were just as busy as ever ...

A woman is doing her Christmas shopping when a shop assistant notices she has a TV remote control in her pocket.

'Do you always carry your TV remote with you to the shops?' asks the assistant.

'No,' says the woman, 'but my husband refused to come and help me, so I thought this was the cruellest thing I could do to him without breaking the law.'

A woman is doing her Christmas shopping. She sees a woollen sweater that she likes but can't believe the price.

She asks the shop assistant, 'Has this jumper got the wrong price on it? It says it's £500. I've seen jumpers like this for sale for just £50.'

'Well, you see, madam,' says the shop assistant. 'You can get jumpers like this for £50 but they will be made from recycled wool. This, however, is made from one hundred per cent virgin lambswool.'

'Oh yeah?' says the woman. 'For an extra £450, I'm not bothered about *what* the lambs get up to at night!'

The competition for business in the shopping mall is furious. The owner of a small shop notices a large corporate rival has opened up, right next door to him, and has put up an enormous sign saying: 'BEST CHRISTMAS DEALS!'

The shop owner is then further horrified when another large store opens up on the *other* side of his shop and puts up an even larger sign saying: 'LOWEST EVER CHRISTMAS PRICES!'

The owner of the small shop is in despair until he has a bright idea and puts up the biggest sign of all over his own shop saying: 'MAIN ENTRANCE!'

A little girl is going round a shop trying to find a Christmas present for her grandmother but doesn't know what to get her. Her mummy suggests buying her a nice new pack of handkerchiefs, so the little girl goes off to look. After half an hour she comes back, still empty handed.

'Didn't you find any hankies for granny?' asks her mum.

'I did,' says the girl. 'But in the end I wasn't sure what size her nose was.'

It's late at night at Christmas and a couple are wandering along the high street looking at the window displays still lit up, even though the stores have closed.

The woman stops in front of a jewellery shop and says, 'Oh, look at that beautiful necklace! I'd love to have that for my Christmas present!'

'OK,' says her partner and produces a brick, throws it through the window and takes the necklace.

Further along the road, the woman sees a coat in the window of a clothing store.

'Oh, look at that lovely coat!' she says. 'I'd love to have that for Christmas as well.'

'OK,' says the man and produces another brick, throws that through the clothes shop window and takes the coat.

Further along the high street, the woman stops by a shoe shop.

'Oh, look at those shoes,' she says. 'I'd love to have those for my Christmas present as well.'

'Now come on!' protests her partner. 'What do you think I am? Made of bricks!?'

An old lady is wandering around the local mall doing her shopping for Christmas when a store detective in a jewellers catches her slipping a diamond necklace into her handbag.

'Please don't tell the police,' the old lady begs him, 'I'll tell you what. I'll happily pay for the necklace if you tell me how much it costs.'

'OK,' says the detective. 'That particular one costs £5,000.'

'What?!' says the old lady. '£5,000 for this rubbish? Have you got anything a bit cheaper?'

Trevor has been out doing his Christmas shopping all day. He gets home late and finds his wife waiting for him.

'What happened?' she asks.

'Sorry,' says Trevor. 'I was about to come home but there was this man at the mall who said he'd dropped a £50 note somewhere and couldn't find it. I was stuck there until they finally closed the whole place for the night.'

'So, you were helping him look for it?' says his wife.

'No,' says Trevor. 'I was standing on it.'

A man is sent to the local toy megastore to get the present that his action-movie-mad son desperately wants.

He asks a shop assistant, 'Where do I find the Arnie Schwarzenegger dolls?'

The assistant points to the end of the store and tells him, 'Aisle B, back.'

Vic has ordered a Christmas present from an online retailer, which he will have to pick up from the local Post Office when it arrives. One day his neighbour tells him he's going to the Post Office so Vic asks if he will check if his parcel is there waiting for him yet.

'Of course,' says the neighbour. 'Always happy to help!'

Two hours later, the neighbour is back.

'Did you get a chance to check about my parcel?' asks Vic.

'Oh yes,' says the neighbour. 'It's definitely there now waiting for you.'

Barry is doing his Christmas shopping but gets caught by the store detective in a sports shop when he tries to shoplift a couple of barbells and a set of weights.

'I'm sorry,' says Barry. 'I did it in a moment of weakness.'

A couple go to the shopping centre to do their shopping on Christmas Eve. They find it completely packed and after a few minutes the wife realizes she has lost sight of her husband. She is quite upset because they have a lot of presents and food shopping to do, so she pulls out her mobile phone to call him.

'Where are you?' she snaps when he finally answers.

'Well,' he says, 'you remember that jewellery shop we went into a couple of years ago? The one that had that diamond necklace in the window that you set your heart on? Remember I said we simply couldn't afford it back then but I promised you that, one day, I would go back to that jewellery store and buy you that necklace?'

'Yes,' says the wife, now sobbing with joy. 'I remember that shop.'

'OK,' says the husband, 'so I'm currently sitting in the bar next to it.'

A couple go out on a shopping expedition to buy Christmas presents for one another. The man appears carrying a bag full of vinyl LPs.

'What did you want to get those for?' asks his wife. 'You know we don't have a turntable!'

'Stop complaining,' says the man, 'I didn't say anything earlier on when you bought yourself that bra.'

It's just before Christmas and Ted and Cynthia are going round the shops hand in hand. They bump into another couple, Bert and Gladys.

'It's very sweet,' says Gladys, 'that you walk round the shops hand in hand.'

'We have to,' says Ted. 'If I let go for a second, she'll go off and buy something.'

> **Going round the shops at Christmas is always a race to see which gives out first. Your money or your feet.**

How can you tell which one of your friends got a great bargain while they were doing their Christmas shopping?

Don't worry, they'll let you know.

Fred is going round the supermarket in the middle of all the Christmas rush. When he gets to the till he asks if one of the shop assistants could help carry his shopping out to his car for him. An assistant is duly summoned, and he and Fred set off across the car park.

Finally, they get to Fred's car and he says, 'Sorry to make you carry my shopping like this. To be honest I could probably have done it myself, but I'm afraid I'm a bit of a lazy bastard.'

'Yes, I worked that out,' says the assistant. 'Here's your Mars Bar.'

A man goes into a police station to report a theft. 'I was just doing my Christmas shopping and my wallet was stolen,' says the man.

'Do you have any idea who might have taken it?' asks the desk sergeant.

'It was a couple of girls,' says the man. 'I was coming out of the shopping mall and these two beautiful young girls jumped out of a van wearing skimpy little elf costumes. They said I was the 1,000th customer to visit the mall that day and that I'd won a special prize from Father Christmas. Then they started kissing me and caressing me and said they were going to take me to Father Christmas to get my prize, but it was in a secret location and they'd have to blindfold me. So they put the blindfold on and kept on kissing me the whole time. But then they stopped, and when I took off the blindfold they'd gone and I realized they'd taken my wallet.'

'I see,' says the desk sergeant. 'And when exactly did this take place?'

'Last Thursday,' says the man. 'Twice on Friday. And then again this morning.'

A man comes out of a department store having just finished his Christmas shopping and sees a traffic warden about to write a ticket.

'Oh, come on!' says the man. 'That's not fair! It's Christmas!'

'It doesn't matter that it's Christmas. This car is illegally parked,' says the traffic warden, tearing the ticket off and placing it on the windshield.

'In that case,' says the man. 'I hope you have a thoroughly miserable Yuletide, you mean old sod! And I hope your Christmas tree gets shoved up your backside!'

'Well, if that's your attitude,' says the traffic warden, raising an eyebrow before proceeding to write another ticket and slap it on the windshield on top of the other one.

'And what's that one for?' asks the man.

'Verbally abusing a traffic warden during the course of his work,' says the warden.

'I'll show you verbal abuse,' says the man, and proceeds to call the traffic warden every name under the sun.

But for every name the man calls him, the traffic warden writes another ticket and slaps it on the windshield.

Finally, the man's wife appears out of the store and asks, 'What's going on here?'

'This idiot keeps writing tickets because I keep swearing at him,' says the man.

'What a complete bas ...' says the woman.

The traffic warden begins to write another ticket but before he can finish, the man grabs his wife's arm and says, 'Quick! Our bus has just turned up across the road!'

Two women are queuing up at the local store with their Christmas shopping. 'How long have we been queuing?' asks one.

'I don't know,' says the other, 'but it must be a long time because I can see the staff beginning to put the Easter Eggs out now.'

DEPARTMENT STORE SANTA PET PEEVES

Parents bring their kids to see you so they can complain in person about last year's presents.

Parents taking you aside when you promise to bring their child a very expensive present on Christmas Day.

Parents responding badly when you tell their child 'I'm afraid you deserve nothing this year'.

Discovering the last person to use the beard had a highly contagious skin disease.

Getting insufficient help from those employed to be your little helpers.

Being told you don't look as though you need any padding to play Santa.

The effects of hundreds of obese children sitting on your lap one after the other.

Being told you are in fact too overweight to fit into the store's Santa costume.

Children pulling your beard off then letting the elastic snap it back into your face.

Being spotted in your costume by an ex-partner, neighbour or someone who was on the same drama course as you.

Being told you're not the real Santa but you are recognizable from that time you appeared on *Crimewatch*.

WHAT A LOAD OF OLD WRAP

Ken and Pam are opening their Christmas presents on Christmas morning. When they open them they discover that all the presents they have bought one another are very delicate items and they end up with an enormous pile of bubble wrap.

'What should I do with all this?' asks Ken.

'Oh, just pop it in the corner,' says Pam.

Four hours later Ken is still going.

It's Christmas morning and presents are being given out.

'I have a great psychic skill,' Barry tells his wife. 'I am always able to tell what's hidden inside Christmas wrapping paper.'

'Really?' says his wife.

'Oh yes,' says Barry. 'It's a gift.'

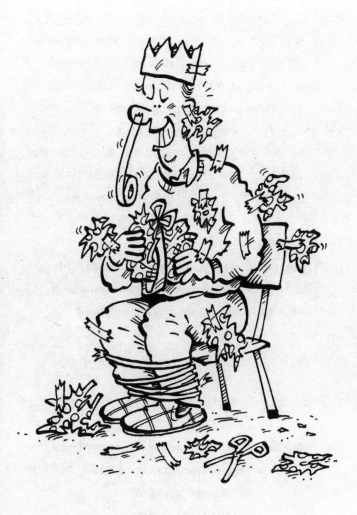

Anyone who seriously believes men are
the equal of women has never seen a man
attempting to wrap a Christmas present.

'I bought my brother some gift-wrap for Christmas.
I took it to the Gift Wrap department and told
them to wrap it, but in a different print so he'd
know when to stop unwrapping.'

STEVEN WRIGHT

**If you can't wrap your Christmas presents
neatly, you should at least try and make it
look like they put up a decent fight.**

'My Christmas wish is to spend more time
unwrapping presents than I do
untangling lights.'

MELANIE WHITE

CUTE LITTLE ANIMALS AREN'T JUST FOR CHRISTMAS

A primary school teacher is teaching her class about things related to Christmas.

She asks a boy in her class, 'Can you name an animal that lives in Lapland?'

'Yes, I can,' says the boy. 'A reindeer!'

'Well done!' says the teacher. 'But can anyone here name another animal that lives in Lapland?'

'Yes, miss!' says another boy, putting his hand up. '*Another* reindeer!'

A man tells a friend that his kids want him to get them a dog for Christmas.

'What sort of dog?' asks his friend.

'They want a Labrador,' says the man.

'Oh no!' says his friend. 'Be careful if you're getting one of those. Have you seen how many of their owners go blind?'

Nigel gets a new dog for Christmas. He phones up his friend Ollie and tells him to come over to have a play with the animal. A few minutes later, Ollie is on the doorstep.

'Before we go inside,' says Ollie, 'do you know if this dog bites?'

'I'm not really sure,' says Nigel. 'In fact, to be honest, the main reason I invited you over here was so I could find out.'

A woman buys her husband a little pug dog as his Christmas present. A few days later her friend asks what he thought about it.

'Well,' says the woman, 'he is very weird looking. He's got an ugly squashed nose, great bulging eyes and rolls of fat all over his body. But luckily the dog seems to quite like him.'

A man is invited to a big Christmas dinner with another family. As they sit to eat, he finds the host's dog won't leave him alone. The dog keeps pawing at him and trying to climb up on his chair to get its head on the table.

'Look at your dog,' says the man to his host. 'He seems to really like me!'

'No,' says the host. 'It's just that we've got so many people here today we ran short of crockery and had to give you his dish.'

A man is looking for a novelty Christmas present to buy for a friend. He goes to an antique shop and begins looking at an impressive pair of stuffed dogs.

'Excuse me!' he calls to the antiques dealer. 'Do you know what those would fetch if they were in good condition?'

'Well,' says the antiques dealer, 'sticks, presumably.'

A little girl asks her mum: 'Mummy, Mummy, can I have a puppy for Christmas?'

'No, you can't,' says mum. 'You'll have turkey like everyone else!'

A man and his young son are walking through the park on a grey winter's day when his dad looks up and points out something interesting in the sky.

'Can you see those geese flying over us, son?' says the man.

'Yes, daddy,' says the little boy.

'And look!' says the man. 'Do you notice how they're all flying in a "v" formation?'

'Yes, daddy,' says the little boy.

'And can you see how one side of the "v" is a bit longer than the other side?' says the man.

'Yes, daddy,' says the little boy.

'And do you know why that is?' says the man.

'No, daddy, I don't,' says the little boy. 'Why is one side of the "v" longer than the other side?'

'It's because,' says the man, 'there are more geese on that side.'

A man is driving through the countryside when an enormous bird pops through the hedge in front of him and races off up the road ahead at great speed. A moment later, a farmer appears and jumps into the car next to the man.

'Follow that turkey!' says the farmer.

'OK! What's going on?' asks the man as they drive off.

'I'm running a genetic experiment on my farm,' explains the farmer. 'We've developed turkeys that all have four legs, so at Christmas the entire family can all get a drumstick.'

'Fantastic!' says the man. 'But do they still taste OK?'

'I don't know,' says the farmer. 'I haven't managed to catch one yet.'

Norma decides to get an exotic pet for her husband's Christmas present. She goes into a pet shop to choose a tarantula, and the owner shows her all the gigantic spiders they have in stock. The cheapest of these, however, costs £500.

'Oh dear,' says Norma. 'That's a bit expensive for a spider. Do you think I'd find one any cheaper if I got it off the web?'

A man spends years teaching his parrot to speak. In the end not only can the bird speak, it can recite the entire text of Charles Dickens' *A Christmas Carol*. Finally, one Christmas Eve, the man decides to take his parrot to a bar, where he loudly announces to everyone:

'I bet everyone here that this bird can recite the entire text of *A Christmas Carol* by Charles Dickens!'

The clientele are all very interested in this. The man is taken up on his bet and a large stack of money is piled up on the bar.

'Right!' says the man. 'Come on, Polly Parrot! Do *A Christmas Carol* for them! Come on, Polly! I'll start you off. "Marley was dead ..."'

But for some reason, this time the parrot doesn't perform the rendition that he has spent years training it to do and instead remains completely silent. Later, back at home, the man is furious as he has lost a small fortune.

'You stupid feathery git!' he yells. 'What's the matter with you?! After all those years of training! Why did you let me down?! Why couldn't you have recited the text I've spent all this time teaching you?'

'Calm down,' says the parrot. 'Just think

about the odds we're going to get when we go back on Boxing Day!'

Fred, the owner of an animal rescue centre, has his brother come to stay over Christmas. One night his brother goes out drinking and arrives back very drunk. He bursts in and finds Fred attempting to warm up a tiny poor bird he has just saved from freezing to death out in the snow. The brother launches into a raucous drunken song but Fred tells him to keep the noise down.

'Please!' says Fred. 'Not in front of the chilled wren!'

Jackie tells her husband she has bought him an exotic pet for his Christmas present.

'What is it?' he asks.

'It's a chameleon,' she tells him.

'Great!' says her husband looking around the room. 'So where is it?'

'I'm not entirely sure,' says Jackie.

It's the end of the year and a farmer calls up his feed supplier to make an order for the new year. 'I'm sorry,' says the supplier, 'but according to your account you haven't paid us for any of the feed we've delivered to you since the summer. I'm afraid that under the circumstances we can't send out any new consignments until you are able to settle your outstanding bill.'

'You swine!' says the farmer. 'How can you expect me to wait that long?'

During a snowstorm on Christmas Day a farmer looks out at his yard and says to his wife, 'Look at the poor pig out there. It's absolutely freezing. Do you think we should bring the poor animal in here?'

'But it's filthy and it stinks,' says his wife.

'Don't worry,' says the farmer. 'The pig will soon get used to it.'

An old man is spending Christmas on his own when he gets a visit from a friend.

'For Christmas,' says the friend, 'I have brought you the perfect present. It's an amazing tortoise that will do anything you want. He can follow commands. He is even able to speak.'

'That's wonderful,' says the old man, taking the tortoise.

'Why not try him out now?' says the friend.

'OK,' says the old man and puts the tortoise out of the front door telling it: 'Tortoise, go to the shops and get me a newspaper!'

A year passes by and Christmas comes again and the old man remembers the tortoise he was given one year ago.

'Bloody hell! That tortoise is a bit slow,' says the old man. 'I think I better go and look for him.'

He steps out of his front door and is surprised to see his missing pet right there on the garden path.

'You're bloody slow, aren't you?' says the old man. 'You've been gone an entire year. Where's my paper?'

'Well,' says the disgruntled tortoise, 'if you're going to be like that about it, I don't think I'll go at all!'

THE TRUE STORY OF THE NATIVITY

Mary and Joseph arrive in Bethlehem and tell the innkeeper they need to make a video call to some shepherds and wise men who they understand are also on their way there.

'Sorry. That's not possible,' the local tells them. 'I'm afraid there is no Zoom at the Inn.'

'Christmas is a baby shower that went totally overboard.'

ANDY BOROWITZ

A primary school teacher asks her children, 'So, why did Joseph and Mary take Jesus with them to Jerusalem?'

A little boy sticks his hand up and says, 'Please, Miss, was it because they couldn't get a babysitter?'

A teacher reads her class the story of the nativity from the Bible and then asks them to draw pictures of the scene.

She sees that one little boy is drawing Jesus in the manger surrounded by Mary and Joseph. In the background there are three men with white beards, one of whom is carrying a pile of gold, and next to him are a big green-grey monster and a horse.

'What are those meant to be?' asks the teacher.

'It's what you just said about the baby Jesus's gifts from the three wise men,' says the little boy. 'Gold, Frankenstein and a mare!'

A teacher has just read the story of the nativity to her class of children and asked them to draw pictures of the favourite moment they remember. As the children start work, the teacher goes round the classroom looking at what they're doing. One little girl is drawing an aeroplane flying through the sky with four people on board.

'What's that meant to be?' asks the teacher.

'It's what you just told us in the story,' says the little girl. 'It's the flight to Egypt.'

'OK,' says the teacher, 'so that's Mary, Joseph and Baby Jesus on the plane. But who's that fourth person at the front?'

'I would have thought that was obvious,' says the girl. 'That's Pontius – the Pilot.'

*'Those presents the three wise men brought Jesus –
were they for Christmas or his birthday?'*

KARL PILKINGTON

A group of primary school children have been rehearsing their nativity play all through December. Finally, they are ready to perform it in front of all the teachers and parents. The school hall is packed and the play begins. Everything goes according to plan until the scene where the innkeeper tells Mary and Joseph that there is no room at the inn.

At this point, the little girl playing Mary forgets her lines and turns to Joseph and says, 'I told you you should have made reservations!'

Quick as a flash Joseph replies, 'Well, they were bound to be busy – it's Christmas.'

A class at a primary school are talking about Christmas.

A little girl tells the teacher, 'Mary is the mother of Jesus. And Jesus is the lamb of God!'

'Well done. That's very good,' says the teacher.

'So,' says the little girl, 'is that why we say Mary had a little lamb?'

What did the Virgin Mary say when she saw the wise men?

'Typical, you wait all day for one then three come along all at once.'

When Mary had a baby boy, the wise men were not surprised ... but you should have seen their faces when she had the little lamb!

At school a class of children are asked to draw pictures of the nativity scene. The teacher goes round looking at what they are doing. One child has drawn the manger with Mary, Joseph and baby Jesus but the teacher is confused to see the figure of a fat man standing at the back of the stable.

'Who's that?' asks the teacher.

'You know him! He's the one from the song,' says the child. 'Round John Virgin!'

Originally in the Bible story there were four wise men. We don't hear very much about the fourth, however, because he was the one on the journey to Bethlehem who said: 'Hold on, guys! I think I might know a shortcut!'

The three wise men turn up in Bethlehem. They go to the stable where Jesus has been born and the first wise man steps up with his gift of gold. Then the second steps forward with his gift of frankincense. Finally, the third wise man speaks out and says: 'But wait, there's myrrh!'

A nativity play is put on at a primary school in Beverly Hills, California. It's fairly traditional, except the story now involves two kids dressed as Mary and Joseph on their way to the inn in Bethlehem while on the other side of the stage, a boy dressed as a shepherd is using his mobile to call for reservations.

In the school art lesson before Christmas the teacher asks her class to draw a picture of the nativity scene. She goes round to see what all the children are drawing and finds one little girl drawing Mary, Joseph and Jesus in the stable. She then starts drawing a figure up in the sky.

'Who's that?' asks the teacher.

'God,' says the little girl.

'Ah,' says the teacher. 'Well, nobody knows what God looks like.'

'They will in a minute,' says the little girl.

The local planning department decide to put on a nativity play but unfortunately their attempts turn out to be unsuccessful for a couple of reasons.

Firstly, no one was able to find three wise men anywhere in the building. And secondly the organizers also had no luck finding a virgin.

On the plus side, they had no problem finding enough asses to fill the stable ...

Just before the Christmas holidays, a primary school teacher asks her pupils what they know about Jesus.

One says, 'I know he was born in a manger.'

'Very good,' says the teacher.

'I know the wise men came and brought gold, frankincense and myrrh,' says another child.

'That's correct as well,' says the teacher.

'And I know he doesn't know how to drive but he owns an Audi,' says another.

'Where did you get that idea?' asks the teacher.

'From my daddy,' says the child. 'We were driving along and an Audi suddenly pulled in front of us and my dad shouted, "Jesus Christ! Why don't you learn how to drive?!"'

IT'S PARTY TIME!

Dave phones up his neighbour Tom and says, 'For Christmas this year my wife and I have decided to have a huge wife-swapping party at my house. We're inviting you and your wife and all the other couples who live on the street.'

'Oh, no,' says Tom. 'I don't think that's my kind of thing at all.'

'OK,' says Dave. 'We'll cross your name off the invite list then.'

Doris is getting ready for a Christmas party.

She asks her husband, 'Do you think this dress makes my bum look big?'

'No,' he says, 'I think it's more likely to be all the mince pies and glasses of Baileys you've been having.'

Bill and his wife, Daphne, go to a Christmas party but end up having a terrible argument in front of everyone when he gets drunk and abusive.

Daphne keeps telling him, 'You promised me it was my turn to get drunk and abusive tonight!'

'What I don't like about office Christmas parties is looking for a job the next day.'

PHYLLIS DILLER

Frank is at a Christmas party when he spots an attractive woman and goes over to chat to her.

'Don't look over there,' he tells her. 'But standing next to the punchbowl is, I think, the ugliest man I've ever seen in my life.'

'Actually,' says the woman, 'that's my husband.'

'Oh, my God!' says Frank. 'I'm so sorry!'

'You're sorry!!' says the woman.

At a Christmas party, a man is hovering underneath the mistletoe.

He asks a passing woman, 'Excuse me. Do you kiss with your eyes closed?'

'I would if I were kissing you,' says the woman.

At the end of a Christmas party, a boy asks a girl, 'Are you the one I was kissing earlier at the party?'

'I'm not sure,' says the girl. 'What time did you get there?'

There is nothing more irritating than finding you've not been invited to a Christmas party that you wouldn't be caught dead at.

At a Christmas party, Jim introduces his new girlfriend to his friend, Bob.

Later at the bar, Jim says, 'She's really good looking, isn't she?'

'Well,' says Bob, 'if you think she's beautiful, you ought to see my new girlfriend!'

'Oh yeah?' says Jim. 'So, she's even better looking is she?'

'No,' says Bob. 'She works for Specsavers.'

At a Christmas drinks party, old Uncle Ernie finds himself cornered by a man trying to sell him life insurance. Ernie keeps protesting that he doesn't need any, but the man is very insistent he considers taking out a policy.

In the end Ernie tells him, 'I'm ninety-eight years old, you know.'

'Blimey!' says the insurance man. 'That is old. I'll tell you what. Why don't you just sleep on it. And then if you wake up, give me a call.'

Brenda goes to a wild Christmas party where there is all manner of drink and drugs on offer. The next morning, she wakes up and finds herself in bed with a really ugly man. She breathes a sigh of relief, safe in the knowledge she's made it safely home to her husband.

For his Christmas party Keith puts up a big marquee in his back garden, with a shiny dance floor, glitter balls, flashing lights and a DJ playing the soundtrack to *Saturday Night Fever*. His guests ask why he's done it at this time of year, when the weather is freezing, but he tells them, 'It's the winter of my disco tent.'

Norman's mum launched her career as a fire-eater halfway through her Christmas party. She hadn't meant to, she was just about to put some more coal on the fire when she tripped over the Christmas tree.

At Christmas one year a group of forty-year-old men decide to meet up. They look around for somewhere to go and eventually settle on their local branch of Hooters because, they say, the waitresses have fantastic bodies and wear tight shorts and skimpy vests.

Ten years later – all now fifty – they decide to meet up again for another Christmas get-together. They look around for somewhere to meet before deciding on Hooters because they can get a drink along with some decent food.

When Christmas comes around ten years later – now aged sixty – they once again look around for somewhere to meet before settling on Hooters because it offers great value for money.

Ten years later – aged seventy – they all get in touch again and try to decide where they should meet up this Christmas. Eventually they decide on Hooters as it has wheelchair access and a toilet for the disabled.

Ten Christmases later, they're now all in their eighties. Once again, they look around for somewhere they can meet ... before eventually settling on Hooters because they've never been there before.

In the last week of term before the Christmas holidays, three students go out to a big party and are late for the next day's lectures. Their teacher asks what happened and they say they got held up because they had a flat tyre.

'OK,' says the teacher. 'We'll start today with a simple thirty-second test. I want you all to sit separately and write down the answer to one question: "Which tyre was it?"'

THE MOST STRESSFUL TIME OF YEAR

It's Christmas Eve and a man gets in from work at five o'clock and calls, 'Hi, honey! I'm home!'

Unfortunately, he then finds his wife is in a foul mood with all the stresses of preparing for Christmas. He tries to calm her down every way he can, but nothing works. Instead, she keeps getting more and more wound up.

After three hours of this, the man has had enough and so he says, 'I hate this bickering all the time. We need to calm down. So, I'll tell you what I'm going to do. I'm going to go out of the front door and then I'll come back in a few seconds later and we'll start the evening all over again.'

His wife agrees that this is a sensible idea, so out he goes and then, a few seconds later, he opens the front door and again calls brightly, 'Hi, honey! I'm home!'

Immediately his wife responds: 'Where the bloody hell have you been? It's after eight o'clock on Christmas Eve and you've only just got back from work!'

The pressures of getting ready for Christmas prove so much for Tony that he ends up with a terribly sore throat and has to go and see his doctor.

The doctor examines him and has a look inside his mouth and says: 'There is quite a lot of abrasion around the back of your throat. Have you eaten anything unusual lately?'

'Well,' says Tony, 'I know this will sound odd, but last night I felt so stressed about Christmas that I ended up chewing on my decorations and in the end I'd eaten all the strips of shiny foil off my Christmas tree.'

'Oh well, that's it then,' says the doctor. 'You're suffering from tinselitis!'

As ever, the Christmas holiday proves to be a very stressful time and by the end of the week, Jane has had enough. She tells her husband, 'I want a divorce.'

'OK,' says her husband, 'but only if you can sum up the reason for me in two words!'

'Very well,' says Jane. 'Our marriage!'

A couple are getting blind drunk at Christmas and begin yelling at each other.

'You hate the sight of me when I'm drunk, don't you?' says the man.

'So what?' says his partner. 'You hate the sight of *me* when you're sober!'

A man is in the pub drowning his sorrows. He tells a fellow drinker, 'I emailed my wife to say I'd be home in time for Christmas but when I got in, I found her upstairs in bed having sex with my best friend. How can anyone be so cold and unfeeling?'

'It's Christmas, so be charitable!' says his fellow drinker. 'Maybe your email ended up in her spam folder.'

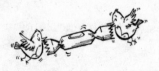

Dennis takes his friend Gordon for a drink after work on Christmas Eve. Dennis has been troubled all year because he has known that

Gordon's wife has been having an affair but up until now he hasn't been able to think of any way of breaking the news.

He buys Gordon a drink and asks him, 'Have you ever thought how sexy it would be to have a threesome?'

'Oh yes,' says Gordon. 'To be honest that's my secret sexual fantasy!'

'Well, I've got good news for you,' says Dennis. 'If you drink up quickly and hurry straight home, you could be in time for the Christmas experience of your life.'

After Christmas a man tells his friend that he and his wife have decided to get a divorce.

'We're going to split the house between us,' says the man.

'Oh yes,' says his friend. 'And which half are you getting?'

'The outside,' says the man.

A little girl comes back from school sobbing one day and tells her family: 'I'm not a virgin anymore!'

Hearing this, every member of the family becomes extremely upset. Her dad starts shouting at his wife that it's all her fault because she's always flirting and messing around with other men. Next, he moves on to their elder daughter whom he blames for setting a bad example by having so many different boyfriends. After this, her mum starts shouting back at her father because he's always being too friendly with other women and looking at dodgy sites on the internet. In the end, the older daughter tells the pair of them to stop yelling and calm down while she asks her little sister what exactly happened.

'What was it?' she asks. 'Was it an older boy at school who took advantage of you?'

'No, it was nothing like that,' says the little girl. 'It was my teacher. She decided to change who was playing who in our nativity play. So, I'm not a virgin anymore. I'm the donkey by the manger instead.'

A man tells his friend, 'I think I'm going to have to divorce my wife! She didn't speak to me during the entire Christmas break.'

'Well,' says his friend, 'I don't think you should rush into anything. You know women like that are extremely hard to find.'

Ron and Bev are having an argument about which of their families they are going to spend Christmas Day with. The bickering rages on for hours until Ron says, 'We're getting nowhere here. It's obvious you like your family and hate all of mine!'

'That's not true at all,' yells Bev. 'I like your mother-in-law much more than I like mine!'

A teacher is talking to her class about families. 'Can you give me an example of two people you know who have a stable relationship?'

A little girl puts her hand up and says, 'Mary and Joseph!'

A man gets home early from work at Christmas only to discover his wife in bed with another man.

'Right! That's it!' says the man, whipping the sheets off the lovers. 'Get out of the bed, the pair of you! I'm going to kill him for this!'

'Wait!' says his wife. 'Before you do anything, do you remember the red sports car I gave you for Christmas last year? That was a present from this man. So are these new golf clubs I got you for Christmas. And so is the skiing holiday we're going on next week. And do you remember when I had that win on the lottery that paid off our mortgage? Again, really it was all from him.'

The man considers for a moment and then tells her: 'Right! Well, don't just stand there, woman! Cover this poor man up before he starts getting cold.'

It's 24 December and a man decides to leave his local bar so his wife won't be annoyed that he didn't spend the evening before Christmas with her. When he gets home, however, he finds his wife in bed with another man.

He goes back to the bar and tells the barman his story. 'Oh no, that's awful,' says the barman. 'What are you going to do?'

'Well,' says the man. 'They didn't see me, so I snuck back out and as they were only just getting started, I reckon I've just got time for a couple more beers.'

On Christmas afternoon Carol tells her husband, 'I found my first grey hair earlier today.'

'Oh dear,' says her husband. 'Was it on your head ... or anywhere else?'

'Neither,' says Carol. 'It was in the stuffing you made for the turkey.'

Les and Fiona are walking past their neighbours' house at Christmas. They see a couple inside opening their Christmas gifts. The man tears open his present then jumps around with joy, before kissing and hugging his partner with gratitude.

'Look at that man in there!' says Fiona. 'He's so happy and grateful for everything. He keeps hugging and kissing his wife and telling her thank you. Why can't you do that occasionally?'

'Don't be ridiculous,' says Les, 'I barely know the woman!'

Mum and dad don't know what to do with their son. Over the past year he has accidentally set fire to their garage, broken three windows in the house while he was playing football in the garden and managed to bring down the ceiling in the living room by jumping on his bed upstairs.

In the end dad says, 'I think for his Christmas present, we should get him a bike.'

'How's that going to help with his terrible behaviour?' asks mum.

'It won't,' says dad. 'But it might help spread it over a wider area.'

On Christmas Day Chas and Bertha discover their daughter crying. It turns out she has been seeing a married man and is now pregnant. Chas is furious and summons the boyfriend round to give him a piece of his mind. The boyfriend, however, turns out to be a very wealthy local businessman.

'I apologize sincerely,' he says. 'As I am already married, I am afraid I am unable to marry your daughter, but in the spirit of Christmas I am prepared to pay your daughter £25,000 child support every month from the birth of the child and to buy you all a new car as compensation for the trouble I've put you to.'

'OK. But what happens if there's a miscarriage?' asks Bertha. 'Do we have to give you the car back?'

'Oh dear. I'm not sure what I'd do in that case,' says the man.

'You could have another go,' suggests Chas.

One Christmas, Gary and Vera find they end up arguing so much that they realize they have to come to an agreement. In the end, they decide that if an argument ever kicks off between them again, they will immediately take time out away from each other. Vera will go into the kitchen and Gary will go out into the garden.

This all works quite well, although Gary does end up spending most of the next year essentially homeless.

Santa and his wife decide they want to spilt up. They search around but none of the lawyers in the North Pole specialize in divorce. Nevertheless, one solicitor they visit says he has something that might help them and hands over a piece of paper with a semicolon printed on it. Santa says he cannot see that this is any use at all.

'But it's just what you need,' says the solicitor. 'You can use it to separate independent Clauses.'

On the weekend before Christmas, Bill stays out partying and playing golf with his friends and manages to spend all of his and his wife's Christmas savings. When he finally gets home on Christmas Eve, he is confronted by his wife, who yells at him for over an hour about what he has done.

Finally, she says, 'So how would you like it if you didn't see me for two or three days over Christmas?'

'Well, after all that tirade,' says Bill, 'I think that would be absolutely fine for me.'

So, Christmas Day came and he didn't see his wife, then Boxing Day and he still didn't see her and then the day after Boxing Day was the same.

Finally, by New Year the swelling began to go down just enough for him to see her again out of the corner of his left eye.

Just before Christmas, two men are in a bar talking. One says to the other, 'I got a massive telling off from my wife just because I threw a snowball at our son.'

'That's terrible,' says the other.

'I know,' says the first, 'and that's not all. The doctor banned me from the maternity ward as well.'

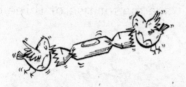

A man wakes up on Christmas morning and discovers that his wife has stuffed all his Christmas presents into a condom instead of a Christmas stocking.

'What's this for?' asks the man.

'I was going to give you a pile of coal,' says his wife, 'but that didn't seem sufficient to tell you how badly you'd screwed up this year.'

Ged and Harry are having a drink a few days after Christmas.

'For Christmas,' says Ged, 'my wife let me do something I'd always dreamed of doing.'

'Oh yeah?' says Harry. 'What was that?'

'She let me win an argument,' says Ged.

CHRISTMAS GIFTS YOUR PARTNER MAY NOT APPRECIATE

A framed portrait of your previous partner.

A framed portrait of your next partner.

A gift voucher for cosmetic surgery.

Any present that is really intended for you rather than them.

A do-it-yourself liposuction kit.

A specially personalized gift engraved with the wrong name.

A specially personalized gift engraved with their name but spelt incorrectly.

Sexy, frilly lingerie – particularly if your partner is a man.

Cleaning products for the house.

Anything with a prominent discounted price label stuck on it.

Anything that they will know you are re-gifting – particularly if it's the present they gave you last Christmas.

A framed portrait of yourself standing next to your previous and next partners.

THE EXPENSE OF IT ALL

Two men are in a bar at New Year talking.

'So, what did you get for Christmas?' asks one.

'Same as I get every year,' says the other. 'Even deeper in debt.'

A woman tells her husband, 'This year, to save money I think we should set a strict limit on how much we spend on each other for Christmas.'

'That's a good idea,' says the husband.

'I'm glad you agree,' says the wife. 'In that case, it's £25 on you and £1,000 on me.'

I wouldn't say Harry was mean, but last Christmas Eve he fired a pistol in the garden and told the kids Santa had committed suicide.

Old Bert is telling his grandchildren about Christmas in the old days.

'People spend thousands on Christmas these days,' says Bert, 'but it wasn't like that when I was a nipper. I would be sent down to the high street with just a few shillings to get all our decorations and food and presents and our Christmas tree and I'd still come back with plenty of change. I'm not able to do that anymore now. And do you know why?'

'No,' say his grandchildren. 'Why?'

'It's because they've put up CCTV in all the high street shops,' says granddad.

Money isn't everything, but at least it encourages your relatives to stay in touch each Christmas.

A couple are going round a big department store doing their Christmas shopping. They decide to split up for an hour so they can each visit their favourite departments and then meet up again at the entrance.

The husband goes round a few floors then stands waiting for his wife at the entrance. Finally, she turns up an hour late, carrying a dozen bags filled with expensive presents for the entire family.

'I don't believe it!' says the man. 'Have you really bought all that?'

'Well, yes, I have,' says the woman, gesturing back into the interior of the shop. 'But look on the bright side. Just look at all the stuff I've left behind.'

A man tells a friend that to save money last year, he told his kids that there was no Father Christmas.

'What are you going to do this year?' asks his friend.

'I'm going to tell the wife,' says the man.

Graham is a terrible miser and his family spend Christmas complaining that he won't spend any money on anything. In the end he tells them, 'OK. As soon as Christmas is over, I'm going to take £10,000 out of the bank for a two-week holiday.'

The rest of the family all cheer until he continues: 'And then, when it's finished its two-week holiday, I'm going to put it all back again!'

A woman tells her husband that she's sick of his cheap Christmas presents.

'This year on Christmas morning,' she tells him, 'I want to see something in the driveway that will go from 0 to 200 in less than 60 seconds!'

Christmas comes and the woman wakes up very excited to see what her husband has bought her. She rushes downstairs and finds her husband at the door with a big smile on his face pointing her towards the driveway.

She runs straight out, squealing with excitement, until she finds sitting there in the middle of the driveway wrapped in Christmas paper, a new set of bathroom scales.

A teenager asks his dad, 'What are you getting me for Christmas this year?'

'Well,' says dad, 'you're getting a bit older now, so we thought we'd get you something really valuable.'

'OK,' says the boy. 'How about a Bitcoin?'

'A Bitcoin?' says dad. 'Wow! Let me just look up online how much they cost.'

Dad pulls up some information on his computer and exclaims: 'What the hell?! These things cost even more than I thought. Some of them are priced at £45,237! And do you know how long it takes me to earn £31,479? One day you'll start work yourself and then you'll know just how much £63,981 really is! Besides I don't really understand what you're going to do with a £26,109 bitcoin anyway. Why not choose something else. To be honest with you £4,807 for a bitcoin was a lot more than we were intending to spend!'

It's coming up to Christmas and a man is suffering terrible financial problems. In the end he is so short of cash and desperate that he decides to go to church, where he gets down on his knees and prays aloud: 'Oh Lord God, please help me. I have no money at all to buy Christmas presents for my children or my dear wife. In your mercy, oh Lord, please could you arrange it for me so that I win the lottery?'

A few days later the man watches the lottery draw but he wins nothing. He goes back to church and again prays to God: 'Oh Lord God, I have lost my job, I can't afford to pay the bills and if I don't get some money soon things are going to be very difficult this Christmas. Please, oh Lord, could you fix it so I win the lottery?'

But again, lottery night comes around and the man is not lucky. So back he goes to church yet again and prays: 'Oh Lord God, they've taken my car away and now I'm going to have my house repossessed. Please show mercy and help me win the lottery to save Christmas for my family.'

But come lottery night, he again fails to win anything. He returns to church and again prays aloud: 'It's almost Christmas Day now, Lord. I'm bankrupt, my house has been repossessed and my car has been taken away. My family is now living on the street. Why will you not hear my prayers to you, oh Lord. Why will you not fix it for me so I win the lottery?'

Suddenly there's a flash of light, the heavens open and God reveals himself to the man and tells him: 'I'm doing all I can. But could you not at least try and meet me halfway and buy yourself a ticket?!'

Chas grew up in a family so poor that at Christmas all they had to exchange was glances.

A few weeks before Christmas. a man tells his friend, 'My wife's credit card has been stolen and she needs it to go and do her Christmas shopping.'

'Have you reported the theft to the police?' asks his friend.

'I would do,' says the man, 'but at the moment the thief is spending less than my wife does.'

Harry was brought up in a very poor family. When he was growing up they couldn't afford a Christmas tree, they just had to make do with a Christmas stump.

A mean man and his wife and children are out doing their Christmas shopping. They end up with so many bags they realize they will have to get a taxi home.

The man hails a cab and asks the driver, 'If you turn your meter off, how much will you charge to drive us home?'

'Well,' says the cabby, 'it will be £15 for you and your wife. But because it's Christmas I won't charge you anything at all for your kids. How about that?'

'Thanks! That's great!' says the mean man and then turns to his kids: 'Right! You lot jump in the taxi with this nice man who has said he'll drive you home while your mum and me go and catch the bus!'

A priest gets a call from a man at the tax office.

The man asks him, 'Do you know a Thomas Callaghan?'

'Oh yes,' says the priest. 'He's one of my parishioners.'

'OK,' says the man from the tax office. 'We need to check about a charitable Christmas donation of £50,000 that Mr Callaghan claims to have made to your church. Can you look in your records and confirm to us that you have received a donation of this amount in the last few weeks.'

'There's no need to check,' says the priest. 'If he's not made the donation already, he certainly will have done by this time tomorrow.'

A week after Christmas, Barry sends a message to all the members of his family: 'Hope you all enjoyed the books I got you for your Christmas presents. Just a gentle reminder: they're due back at the library tomorrow.'

When he was little, Frank was so poor he didn't get a yo-yo when he asked for one at Christmas. His parents could only afford to buy him a yo.

With the recent steep increases in the price of fuel, Gordon has become very concerned about his heating bill. He tells his kids that in order to avoid letting in any cold drafts, they mustn't even open the windows on their advent calendars.

Bill has started putting his money into a special Christmas club saving scheme. It helps you save up your money through the year so you can afford to pay for last year's presents.

Christmas is in our hearts twelve months every year. And thanks to the amount it costs us, it's on our Visa card statements for just as long as well.

Colin is called in to see his bank manager first thing in January. The bank manager tells him an interesting fact: 'Did you know the Chinese have a strict rule to settle all their debts on New Year's Day?'

'Well, that's all very well,' says Colin, 'but the Chinese don't have Christmas the week before their New Year!'

After all the expense of Christmas Bert has a good talk with his wife about her extravagant shopping habits. As a result, they agree there have to be some changes. He's giving up drinking from 1 January.

POST EARLY FOR CHRISTMAS

A man goes into the Post Office and asks the assistant for a box 5 centimetres high, 5 centimetres wide and 50 metres long.

'What do you need that for?' asks the assistant.

'I've bought my brother a garden hose for his Christmas present,' says the man, 'and now I need to post it to him.'

A woman says to her husband, 'Should we give the postman some money for Christmas?'

'No. He's already had enough round here,' says the husband. 'Apparently he's slept with every woman on this street, apart from one.'

'I know!' says the wife. 'And I bet it's that stuck-up cow at number 17.'

The postman is very busy over Christmas but he keeps getting attacked on his rounds by a dog. Eventually the Post Office call up the dog's owner and ask him, 'Can you stop your dog attacking the postman on his bike?'

'That's completely ridiculous,' says the man. 'It can't be my dog. He doesn't even know how to ride a bike.'

The postman knocks at a door and asks the owner, 'What about a Christmas tip?'

'OK,' says the homeowner. 'Never catch snowflakes with your tongue until the birds have gone south for the winter.'

Walter takes a parcel to the Post Office to send it to a relative for their Christmas present. The Post Office assistant checks the parcel and tells him, 'I'm afraid this item is too heavy. You're going to have to put some more stamps on it.'

'OK,' says Walter. 'But how is that going to make it less heavy?'

'Mail your packages early so the post office can lose them in time for Christmas.'

JOHNNY CARSON

A teenager is doing Christmas work with the Post Office and is out delivering mail. When he delivers the post to one house, the owner comes out and says, 'I hope you're not expecting a tip because it's Christmas. I never give one.'

'That's OK,' says the teenager. 'The guys in the sorting office warned me that you never give anything. They think you must be a bit short of money.'

'Oh, do they now?!' says the man, pulling out a £20 note and handing it over to the teenager. 'Well, you can just tell the guys in the sorting office that I gave you this.'

'Thank you. I will,' says the teenager. 'And I'll put this money towards my college fund.'

'Very good,' says the man. 'And what is it you're studying?'

'Psychology,' says the teenager.

On a freezing cold winter morning, a postman is doing his rounds. As he delivers his Christmas cards, he comes to a house but finds they have so much post that it won't fit in the letterbox. He knocks on the door and a beautiful woman stands staring at him.

The postman says, 'I'm sorry to bother you but I couldn't fit all your post in the letterbox. So here it is.'

'Thank you,' says the woman and then adds, 'It looks freezing out there. Why don't you come in for a rest?'

The postman thanks her and steps inside. Once the door has closed, the woman says, 'I've got an idea. Why don't we go upstairs and have sex!'

The postman can't believe what is happening but follows her upstairs anyway. Later they come back down and the postman tells her, 'That was fantastic but I better get back to my round.'

'Don't be silly,' says the woman. 'Come and have some breakfast before you go!'

She opens the door to the kitchen and reveals a table laid out with food.

After the meal, the postman says, 'Right! I really had better go!'

The woman says, 'Well, thank you very much for everything.' And with that she hands him two pounds.

The postman is confused and asks, 'What is going on here? You invite me in, you have sex with me, you make me a lovely breakfast and then you give me two pounds?'

'Well, to be honest,' says the woman, 'really it was all my husband's idea. I asked him what sort of Christmas tip we should give the postman and he said, "Screw him! Just give him a couple of quid!" But the breakfast was my idea!'

While at the Post Office to get some stamps for his Christmas cards, Sid finds himself stuck in a queue behind the devil.

'Why did he take so long?' asks Sid when he gets to the counter.

'Well, you know how it is with him,' says the assistant. 'He can take many forms.'

On Christmas Eve, Linda surprises the postman by opening the door completely naked.

It's not certain what shocked the postman the most: the fact that Linda was in the nude, or the fact that she knew where he lived.

A delivery man knocks on Albert's door with a large Christmas present in his hand.

'I can't tell if this parcel is supposed to be for you or not,' says the delivery man. 'The name on it is smudged.'

'That's not for me then,' says Albert. 'My name's Perkins.'

In the run-up to Christmas everyone in the street is receiving lots of items ordered online. One afternoon a delivery man knocks on Vince's door and says, 'I've got a parcel for your neighbour.'

'Right,' says Vince, 'in that case you've got the wrong house, haven't you?'

Clive tries sending his brother a Bon Jovi album for his Christmas present. He keeps checking if it has been delivered yet but the tracking report only ever says: 'Oh wo, it's halfway there ...'

A delivery driver comes up the path dragging an enormous parcel and knocks on the front door of the house.

When the door opens he says, 'Special surprise Christmas delivery for Widow Jones!'

The woman at the door says, 'I'm not Widow Jones, I'm Mrs Jones.'

'Well, you say that,' says the delivery man, 'but you haven't seen what's inside this parcel yet.'

TIME TO GO TO CHURCH

During his sermon in the Christmas morning service, the vicar notices that one of the old ladies in the congregation has fallen asleep and the sound of her snoring is distracting everyone else.

'Excuse me,' calls the vicar to the man sitting next to her. 'Could you wake that old lady up, please?'

'I don't see why I have to,' says the man. 'You're the one who sent her to sleep.'

The congregation are filing out of church on Christmas day after the morning service.

'Thank you, vicar,' says one man as he comes out. 'Your sermon this morning reminded me of the peace and love of God!'

'That's very nice to hear,' says the vicar. 'Was it because it covered the story of the first Christmas?'

'No,' says the man, 'it was because it passed all understanding and it endured forever!'

A mum is trying to get her young son to come to church on Christmas Day.

'We have to go to church today,' says his mum, 'because today is Jesus's birthday.'

'I don't see why,' says the boy. 'He didn't come when it was mine.'

On Christmas Eve a young couple appear at a priest's door and say they want him to marry them right there and then.

'No. I'm sorry. That's completely impossible at the moment,' says the priest. 'It's Christmas and I'm far too busy. You'll have to book the church properly for some time after Boxing Day.'

'Oh no!' says the young man. 'I'll tell you what, father, in that case, could you just say a few words to tide us over the next couple of days?'

A little boy goes to church with his grandparents on Christmas morning. The family are all going in when the boy notices a board inscribed with the names of different people and surrounded by photos of young men in uniform.

'What's this?' asks the boy.

'Those are all the boys who came to this church who died in the service,' says his grandfather.

'Oh God!' says the boy. 'Was that the carol service on Christmas Eve or this Christmas Day service?'

A little boy is taken to church to make his confession before Christmas Day. He is told by the priest that he has to say three Hail Marys for his penance.

'I don't know how I'm going to do that,' says the boy. 'I only know one.'

A little boy is watching his father, the vicar, writing his sermon for the Christmas Day service.

The boy asks, 'How do you know what to put in your sermon?'

'God tells me!' says the vicar.

'Oh, really?' says the boy. 'Well, you can't be listening very hard because you keep having to cross things out!'

A rabbi and a priest are having a drink together over Christmas and Hanukkah and begin talking about the perks of their different jobs.

The priest says, 'I've got this lovely cosy rectory to live in, with the fire blazing and a housekeeper and a cook to look after me and make my Christmas dinner. And it's all paid for by the church!'

'Well, that's all very well,' says the rabbi, 'but do you think you will ever be promoted?'

'I might be,' says the priest. 'Next year I could be appointed to be a bishop for example.'

'And is that as high as you could go?' asks the rabbi.

'No,' says the priest. 'Maybe in a few years I could become an archbishop.'

'And is that as high as you could go?' asks the rabbi.

'No,' says the priest. 'I could eventually be invited to go to Rome and serve as a cardinal.'

'And what about beyond that?' asks the rabbi.

'Well,' says the priest, 'it would be a very rare honour but it's not impossible I could one day be appointed the Pope, the head of the entire Catholic Church.'

'And is that it?' asks the rabbi.

'Yes! Well, what do you think I could do beyond that?' snaps the priest. 'They're not going to promote me to be God, are they?!'

'You say that,' says the rabbi, 'but one of our boys was.'

At Christmas a priest calls round to see an old lady in his parish. She sits him down in the living room then goes to fetch him a cup of tea and a mince pie. While she is away in the kitchen he notices an electric organ with a book of Christmas carols on the stand and, next to it, a bowl of water with a condom floating in it.

When the old lady returns with his tea, the priest can't help but ask the reason for the floating condom.

'Well,' says the old lady, 'I was doing my Christmas shopping the other week and I saw these little silver packets on display with instructions on the label saying, "Keep moist and put on your organ to avoid disease". So, I thought I'd try one and, do you know, I haven't had a cold since!'

A family go to church on Christmas Day but the service goes on and on.

After the priest has been giving his sermon for over half an hour, the smallest child turns to his mum and says, 'Mum, if we just do the collection and give him his money now, will he let us go home?'

The Queen goes to see the Archbishop of Canterbury at Christmas. The bishop arrives to pick her up from the railway station in a horse and sleigh and they set off through the snow to the cathedral.

Halfway through their journey, the horse suddenly and very noisily breaks wind.

The archbishop is very embarrassed and says, 'I'm so sorry about that.'

'Don't mention it,' says the Queen. 'To be honest, I thought it was the horse.'

At a little church in the countryside only the local farmer turns up for the dawn Christmas morning service. In the circumstances, the vicar asks the farmer if he'd mind if the mass was cancelled and if he could come back instead for the service later in the morning.

'Yes, I would mind!' says the farmer. 'I would never do this in my job. If I go out in the yard with my bucket of corn to feed the hens and only one of them comes, I wouldn't send that hen away hungry.'

The vicar is very moved by the farmer's wise words. 'That's a very good point,' he says, before proceeding to perform the entire dawn service complete with a thirty-minute sermon on how we must not shirk our duties, even at Christmas.

Afterwards the vicar asks the farmer if he enjoyed the service.

'No, I didn't!' says the farmer.

'But,' says the vicar, 'you told me that if you go out in the yard with your bucket of corn and only one hen comes, you will still take the trouble to feed that single hen!'

'I know,' says the farmer. 'But I wouldn't give her the entire bucket, would I?'

'I once wanted to become an atheist but I gave up ...
they have no holidays.'
HENNY YOUNGMAN

In the run-up to Christmas a young vicar goes to the local cathedral to listen to the bishop giving a service in the hope that it will give him some inspiration for his own sermons.

The bishop climbs into the pulpit and begins his sermon, 'I'll always remember the best years of my life. I spent them naked in the arms of a woman who wasn't my wife!'

The congregation are stunned by this opening line and there is an audible gasp before the bishop carries on: 'And do you know who that woman was? It was of course my mother when I was a tiny baby!'

This is so clever that the congregation all burst into laughter and applause before listening intently to the rest of the bishop's sermon.

That was brilliant, thinks the young vicar and he decides to use the same trick when he does his Christmas sermon.

Christmas Day comes round, and the church is completely packed as the young vicar climbs into the pulpit to do his sermon, which he is sure is going to go down as well as the bishop's.

'I'll always remember the best years of my life. I spent them naked in the arms of a woman who wasn't my wife!' the vicar begins telling his congregation.

Unfortunately, he then quickly realizes he can't quite remember how the joke was supposed to go and has to improvise.

'I can't quite remember who that woman was now,' he stammers, 'but I can tell you one thing. The bishop recommends her very highly.'

The Pope comes out of the Vatican on Christmas Day to make a seasonal address to all his followers.

He tells them, 'The almighty and omnipotent Lord, who controls all things on Heaven and Earth, has personally chosen me to lead the one true Holy Roman Catholic Church.'

'OK,' calls a voice from the crowd. 'If that's the case, why did you have to get a lightning conductor installed on the roof of the Vatican?'

It's just after Christmas and a vicar comes out of his church when he hears the intoning of a prayer. He discovers his five-year-old son and his friends have found a dead robin. The children had decided that the poor creature deserved a proper burial, so they had found a small box and dug a hole in the church garden. The vicar's son is given the job of saying the appropriate prayers and so, with great dignity, he intones what he thinks is normally said on these occasions:

'In the name of the Father, the Son, and into the hole he goes!'

A priest is walking through the snow one day just before Christmas when he notices a tiny boy go up to a big house and try to ring the bell. Unfortunately, the boy is so small and the bell is so high up that he cannot reach it.

The priest goes over and says, 'Happy Christmas! Let me help you, my child!'

And with that he reaches across and gives the doorbell a good solid ring. Then the priest crouches down to the boy and says, 'And now what, my little fellow?'

'And now we run like hell!' says the little boy.

Father O'Brien goes to visit his friend Father O'Reilly and is treated to a lovely piece of Christmas cake made by the housekeeper, Mrs O'Riordan. During his visit, Father O'Brien notices how friendly Father O'Reilly and Mrs O'Riordan are and begins to become suspicious about their relationship. To test his theory, he slips the silver cake slice used to serve the Christmas cake into his pocket. A few days after his visit, Father O'Reilly notices that it's missing and tells Mrs O'Riordan that Father O'Brien must have taken it.

'Don't accuse him,' says the housekeeper. 'Just pop a note in with his Christmas card telling him that you're not saying he took the cake slice and you're not saying that he didn't, but it has been missing since his visit.'

A couple of days later, Father O'Reilly gets a Christmas card back from Father O'Brien, inside which he finds a note saying:

'I'm not saying that you are sleeping with Mrs O'Riordan and I'm not saying that you're not, but I'd just like to point out that if you'd been in your own bed any time since my visit you would have found your flipping cake slice by now.'

Following midnight mass on Christmas Eve, a priest stands at the church door shaking hands with his parishioners as they leave.

As one man passes by and proffers his hand, the priest says, 'Ah! Mr O'Dell! It's great to see you here tonight, but I'd really like to see you in church a little more often. Will you not take up the standard and join the Army of God?'

'Oh, but I am in the army of God,' says Mr O'Dell.

'Oh, really?' says the priest. 'So why do we only ever see you here at Christmas?'

O'Dell looks over his shoulder and whispers, 'Because, father, I'm in the Secret Service.'

For his Christmas present the local priest receives a bottle of cherry brandy from Gladys Higginbottom, the oldest lady in the parish.

'You mustn't tell anyone I gave this to you,' says Gladys, 'because I've told everyone for years that I'm a complete teetotaller.'

The priest says he understands completely and so, when the church magazine comes out in

January, the priest has written a line of thanks and appreciation to each of the parishioners who had donated Christmas presents, including one that reads:

'Thanks to Mrs Higginbottom for her kind gift of fruit and the spirit in which it was given.'

On Christmas Day the priest gets up in the pulpit to make an appeal for contributions to help renovate the crumbling old church in the coming new year. As he speaks, he keeps glancing across at the richest man in the parish, who is sitting in the front pew.

Finally, the rich man takes the bait. He stands up and says in front of the entire congregation, 'OK, father. I am prepared to contribute £1,000 to the restoration fund!'

As soon as he speaks there is a rumbling noise and a lump of plaster falls from the ceiling onto his head.

'OK. In fact, I'll make that £2,000!' says the rich man.

And again, just as he speaks, there is a rumbling sound before another bit of plaster falls down and strikes him.

'OK then,' says the rich man. 'I'll contribute £5,000!'

The priest waits for something to happen but this time there is no rumbling sound.

After a few moments, the priest looks up and prays to heaven, 'Come on, Lord! Hit him one more time!'

On Christmas Eve, an old man walks into a church and goes into the confessional.

'Father!' says the old man loudly. 'I'm eighty years old and last night I was in bed with a pair of twenty-year-old twins!'

'That's absolutely disgusting,' says the priest. 'If you're a married man, you have committed adultery.'

'But I'm not married, father,' says the old man. 'My wife passed away ten years ago.'

'It's still disgusting,' says the priest. 'Have you remarried since?'

'No,' says the old man. 'I've lived alone ever since my wife died.'

'It doesn't matter. This is still a terrible sin for a Catholic,' says the priest.

'But I'm not a Catholic,' says the old man. 'I'm an atheist.'

'Well,' says the priest, 'if you're not a Catholic, why on Earth have you come in here to tell me you spent the night with a pair of twenty-year-old twins?'

'I'm telling everyone,' says the old man.

A priest phones up one of his parishioners just before Christmas and a little boy answers and whispers, 'Hello?'

'Hello,' says the priest, 'is your daddy home?'

'No,' whispers the little boy. 'He's very busy at the moment.'

'Well, what about your mummy?' asks the priest.

'No,' whispers the boy. 'She's very busy as well.'

'What about your older brothers and sisters?' asks the priest.

'They're all very busy,' whispers the boy.

'Well, are there any other grown-ups in the house?' asks the priest.

'Yes,' says the boy. 'There's two firemen and a policeman here at the moment. But they're all very busy.'

'OK,' says the priest, 'So you mean you've got your entire family, two firemen and a policeman all in the house, but all of them are too busy to speak to me. What are they all doing?'

'They're looking for me,' whispers the little boy.

A priest is about to set off to spend Christmas in Rome, when one of his parishioners comes to him.

'Bernadette! How are you?' says the priest.

'I'm fine, Father,' says Bernadette. 'But you know my husband and I have been trying to have a baby for the past ten years without any success? I fear we are barren.'

'Don't worry,' says the priest. 'I am going to Rome and I will light a candle for you in St Peter's Basilica and then surely at this time of year when we remember the birth of Jesus, the Lord will look favourably on you.'

Bernadette thanks him and he sets off on his journey.

Five years later, the priest is having his Christmas dinner when there's a knock on the door. Waiting outside is Bernadette's husband.

'Father,' he says. 'Remember that candle you lit for me and Bernadette all those years ago? Well, we now have two sets of twins and a set of triplets and this morning we just found out that Bernadette is pregnant again, this time with quadruplets! So, I got you this.' And with that the husband presents the priest with an all expenses-paid ticket to Rome.

'Oh, that's very kind,' says the priest, 'but you didn't need to get me a thank-you present.'

'It's not a thank-you present,' says the husband. 'We need you to go back to Rome as soon as you can and blow that flipping candle out.'

It's Christmas Eve and a drunk has wandered into a Catholic Church. He walks up the aisle then sees a confessional and goes inside. After a few moments the priest on the other side of the grill, coughs gently to try and attract the drunk's attention but there is no reply.

After another minute the priest knocks loudly on the wall and says, 'Hello?'

Finally, the drunk says: 'Sorry, mate. Can't help you. There's no paper in this cubicle either.'

The head of a big turkey-producing company is included in a papal audience. While he's there he takes the opportunity to put a business proposition to his holiness.

He asks the Pope, 'In the run-up to Christmas, could you change the wording of the Lord's Prayer slightly throughout Advent? Instead of saying "Give us this day our daily bread" could you instead get all your cardinals and bishops and priests and parishioners to say "Give us this day our daily turkey"? In exchange, my company will then donate £50 million to charities of your choice.'

The Pope is appalled at such a suggestion and sends the man away. A few weeks later the man calls the Pope and tells him the offer has been increased to £100 million. The Pope nevertheless once again immediately dismisses any suggestion of changing the Lord's Prayer and tells the man to get off the phone. A few days before the beginning of Advent the man comes back to the Pope with an astonishing offer of £200 million.

The Pope is forced to stop and consider all the good work that could be done with such a large donation. In the end he decides to go ahead.

The next day a special meeting of all the church's cardinals is called for the Pope to tell them about the agreement.

The Pope gets up to address them. 'Well,' he says. 'I have good news and bad news for you. The good news is that the church is about to receive a record donation of £200 million. The bad news is that we have lost the Wonderloaf account.'

The vicar has just finished conducting a Christmas service when a little boy runs up to him.

'When I grow up,' says the little boy, 'I'm going to save up all my money and give it you.'

'That's very nice of you,' says the vicar. 'But why would you want to do that?'

'Because,' says the boy, 'my dad says you're probably the poorest preacher we've ever had here.'

Tom, Dick and Harry are walking past a church late on Christmas Eve. Harry stops to light a cigarette but just as he does so, Tom says, 'Look at that church all lit up. What's going on in there? Let's go in and find out.'

Harry has to put his cigarette out and puts the smouldering butt in his pocket to relight it later. Inside the church, they discover the Christmas midnight mass is being celebrated and sit down in one of the pews.

Just then the priest walks down the aisle asking the congregation, 'Who are the three most important people you should think of at this time of year?'

'Is it my wife and children?' says Tom.

'No, it isn't,' says the priest.

'Is it my parents and my wife?' asks Dick.

'No, it is not,' says the priest, turning to Harry, whose cigarette has just set light to his trousers.

'JESUS, MARY AND JOSEPH!' screams Harry.

'At last we have a winner!' says the priest.

IT'S ON THE CARDS

A man goes to the Post Office to buy some stamps for his Christmas cards. He's hoping for self-adhesive stamps but is instead presented with old-fashioned stamps that need to be licked.

'Oh no,' he says, 'Do I have to stick these on myself?'

'You can if you want,' says the assistant, 'But it'll probably work better if you stick them on the envelopes.'

A woman goes to the Post Office to get some stamps to send her Christmas cards.

'OK,' says the assistant, 'What denominations do you need?'

'Well,' says the woman, checking her cards, 'since you ask: I need twenty Catholic, fifteen C of E, a dozen Methodists and an Episcopalian.'

A boy gets a Christmas card from his mean old uncle. Inside, the message reads: 'Happy Christmas! I didn't know what to get you for your present, so I was going to enclose a cheque for £100 but unfortunately, I sealed the envelope before I remembered to put it in.'

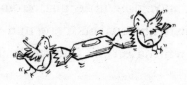

A priest is opening his Christmas cards one morning in December. Some of the cards have personal notes enclosed from his parishioners expressing their thanks for his work during the past year.

One of the cards, however, has been sent anonymously and a note drops out of it with just one word written on it: 'Arsehole!'

On Christmas morning, the priest gets up to address the congregation and tells them, 'Some of you have written me lovely notes expressing your thanks to me. One or two of you wrote the notes but forgot to sign your names on them. And this person,' he says, pulling out the note with the single word written on it, 'has signed his name but forgotten to write the note!'

It's Valentine's Day and for a bit of fun a mum makes a Valentine's card for her little daughter. After she finds it, however, the little girl looks concerned.

'What's the matter?' asks her mother. 'Do you know who your card is from?'

'Well,' says the little girl, 'from analysing the handwriting on this card and comparing it to the writing on my Christmas presents in December, I think my secret admirer might be Father Christmas.'

Daphne sits writing her Christmas cards thinking she should have got cards with self-sealing envelopes rather than ones she has to keep licking to stick down. In the end, the whole experience leaves her with a bad taste in her mouth.

Just before Christmas a man receives a card from his friend. He opens it but discovers the card doesn't have any festive message or picture on it but instead just the letters: 'A B C D E F G H I J K M N O P Q R S T U V W X Y Z.' A few days later the man sees his friend and asks him, 'What was that all about? Why was that card supposed to have anything to do with Christmas?'

'Didn't you get it?' asks the friend. 'No L!'

Two brothers are spending Christmas at their grandmother's. On Christmas morning they open their presents and the younger brother discovers a scarf that his grandma had knitted for him. The older brother, meanwhile, only gets a card saying: 'Merry Christmas, Love Grandma'. Later that night the older brother complains, 'I don't understand it! Why does grandma love you more than she loves me? Every Christmas she gets you a present and I only get a card.'

'That's not true at all,' says the little brother. 'I've seen you get presents!'

'That was years ago when I was little,' says

the older brother. 'These days all I get is cards. In fact, I bet you that next year I will just get a card again.'

'It's a bet then,' says the little brother. 'Let's call it £100.'

'OK,' says the big brother. '£100 says I get a card again next year.'

The next Christmas arrives and this time grandma gives both the brothers presents. The little brother is delighted because now his sibling is going to have to pay him £100.

'Come on!' says the little brother. 'Open your present and let's see what it is.'

The older brother begins peeling off the wrapping paper, revealing a lovely bit of knitwear made by his grandma.

'Is it a scarf?' asks the little brother.

'No. It's something more than that,' says the brother.

'It's a jumper, isn't it?' says the little brother. 'You got a jumper! So now you owe me £100!'

'No, it's not a jumper,' says the older brother pulling out his present. 'And it's you that owes me £100 because, as you can see, grandma has – exactly as I predicted – given me a cardigan!'

An old man doesn't know what he should get for his grandchildren's Christmas presents. He looks around the shops, but he isn't sure what they're interested in or what they might already have. So instead, he decides to send them each a cheque.

He sits down, writes the cheques and then writes the Christmas cards to send each of them. In each card he writes, 'Happy Christmas, love Granddad. PS You can buy your own present this year!'

Finally, he pops them in the post. Christmas comes and goes and he doesn't hear back from any of them and is wondering what has happened, until he discovers in his study under a magazine, the little pile of cheques which he'd forgotten to include with his grandchildren's cards.

GOING OUT FOR CHRISTMAS DINNER

A couple go out for Christmas dinner in a restaurant.

'I reckon,' says the man, 'that this turkey is rather old.'

'What gives you that idea?' says the wife.

'Well,' says the man, 'the fact they had to bring it to our table in a wheelchair for a start.'

Melvyn and his family go out for Christmas dinner. They enjoy a large and completely delicious meal with turkey and all the trimmings, followed by a lovely Christmas pudding. Afterwards they all agree that it has been the best Christmas dinner they have ever had and immediately book a table for the next Christmas.

A year later they return to the restaurant. This time, however, they find themselves being served a grey and insipid meal which looks like leftovers from twelve months ago.

Melvyn complains to the restaurant manager.

'What's going on here?' he asks. 'We ordered exactly the same Christmas dinner as we had last year but this time the meal is really disappointing and unpleasant.'

'Well, you see,' says the manager, 'the thing is, last year you were sitting right by the window.'

Norman tells his family he's taking them out for Christmas dinner at a fancy open-air restaurant.

Norman enjoys himself and the meal is surprisingly inexpensive but the rest of the family can't understand why the restaurant only has soup on the menu and why all the waiters are dressed in Salvation Army uniforms.

A little old couple walk into a restaurant and order a Christmas dinner between them. The food is brought to their table and the little old man carefully divides up all the turkey and sprouts and roast potatoes and places this on a small plate in front of his wife.

Another man, sitting nearby, takes pity on them and offers to get the old lady her own Christmas dinner.

'No thanks, son,' says the old man. 'We always share everything between us.'

The man then notices that the little old lady hasn't touched her food and instead sits watching her husband eat.

The man asks her, 'Are you OK? Why aren't you eating anything?'

'Don't worry about me,' says the old lady. 'I'm just waiting for my go with the dentures.'

A family are having a big Christmas dinner in an expensive restaurant. They have just been served with their Christmas pudding when suddenly the youngest child starts desperately coughing and spluttering.

The mother screams: 'Help! My son is choking! He's just swallowed the sixpence from the Christmas pudding! Someone help us, please!'

A man calmly gets up from a nearby table, walks across, inspects the situation before performing the Heimlich manoeuvre. Then, as the boy sits down again, greatly relieved, the man picks from the floor the silver sixpence that has just been ejected and pockets it.

'Thank you so much,' says the mother. 'You must be a doctor.'

'No,' says the man. 'I work for the Inland Revenue.'

A few days before Christmas a couple decide to go out for a big slap-up Christmas dinner. They arrive at the restaurant but find that it's fully booked and there's no chance of getting served that night.

They try again the next day but once again the restaurant is completely booked up. The same thing happens the next day, and when they try to make a reservation for Christmas Eve, they are told there is no chance of getting a booking before the middle of January.

In desperation they ask if they can book for the following Christmas but it turns out that the restaurant is already fully booked twelve months ahead.

The man is now incandescent with frustration and yells at the manager, 'You know what? You'd do a hell of a lot more business at this restaurant, if it wasn't so busy all the time!'

CHRISTMAS LISTS

Father Christmas is sitting in his grotto at the shopping centre watching all the children waiting outside with their parents. Suddenly, the next in line is a young woman.

'I'm sorry,' says Father Christmas, 'I'm really just here to ask the children what they want for Christmas.'

'No, I'm not here for myself,' says the woman. 'I want to ask you for something for my mother.'

'OK then,' says Father Christmas. 'What is it that your mother would like me to bring her for Christmas?'

'A millionaire son-in-law,' says the woman.

Dad asks his son what he wants for Christmas.

'Google Glasses!' says the boy.

'I don't need to do that, do I?' says dad. 'I already know what glasses are!'

A Christmas parade is coming into town and the event is being covered by the local news. The presenter stands with a group of little children watching as Father Christmas arrives in town and turns to interview them as he goes past.

'Are you going to give Father Christmas your Christmas list?' he asks one little girl.

'No, definitely not,' says the little girl.

'Why not?' asks the reporter.

'Because that's not the real Father Christmas!' she says. 'The real Father Christmas is the one at the shopping centre!'

Bert asks his friend Stan what his wife wants from him for Christmas.

'Oh, she's made the Christmas shopping really easy for me,' says Stan. 'She's asked me to get her a gun, Duct tape, some rope and a large, sturdy bag.'

'That sounds exciting,' says Bert.

'Yes,' says Stan. 'I can't wait to see what she gets me.'

'Christmas is a time when kids tell Santa what they want and adults pay for it. Deficits are when adults tell the government what they want and their kids pay for it.'

RICHARD LAMM

A boy's parents ask him what he wants for Christmas. He tells them, 'I'd like something to wear and something to play with.'

So they buy him a pair of jeans with a hole in the pocket.

For Christmas a young woman tells her boyfriend to buy her some lingerie with a special message embroidered on them.

'What's the message you want?' he asks.

'"If you can read this, you're too close!"' says the girl.

'OK. Do you want that in capitals?' asks the boyfriend.

'No,' says the girl. 'Braille.'

Tom's wife asks him, 'What's the main thing you want for Christmas this year?'

'To be woken up when it's all over,' says Tom.

GIFT EXPERIENCES

For a special Christmas present Clive's wife buys him something he has always wanted: the chance to learn how to skydive.

A few weeks later, he's up in a plane with a group of other men all doing their first ever skydive. The course instructor throws open a hatch on the side of the plane and yells at the men to start jumping out, one after the other. One of the men, however, is very resistant.

'Don't be so pathetic!' says the instructor. 'You've got to overcome your fear! Let me help you!'

And with that, the instructor pushes the man straight out of the plane and sends him plummeting down towards the ground.

'I don't think you should have done that,' says Clive.

'Oh really?' says the instructor. 'Why not?'

'That was the pilot,' says Clive.

For his Christmas present last year Dave's wife bought him an exciting adventure experience and booked him on a week-long survival course.

Sadly, Dave didn't pass.

Ted's wife gets him an exciting adventure experience package for his Christmas present. First thing in the New Year Ted goes out for his special day learning how to sky dive.

The instructor takes Ted up in a plane and says, 'You jump out of the plane first and then I'll jump out after you and we'll go down together.'

Ted jumps out, followed by the instructor. The instructor signals for Ted to pull his ripcord, which he does and his parachute duly opens.

The instructor gives him a thumbs up then pulls his own ripcord. However, the instructor's parachute then fails to open and Ted sees him plummeting down past him towards the ground, desperately trying to get his parachute to open.

'So that's it, is it?!' says Ted, struggling to undo the straps to his own parachute. 'Well, if he wants a race, I'll give him a race!'

Marvin is delighted with his Christmas present from his wife. She has got him a gift experience that will enable him to fulfil his lifetime's dream of being able to drive a train.

It cost her quite a lot of money but it still worked out slightly cheaper than his usual off-peak return.

Belinda talks her husband into buying her a beauty treatment for her Christmas present. She goes to the beautician and comes back two hours later.

'Blimey!' says her husband. 'How much is this all going to cost me?'

'I don't know yet,' says Belinda. 'I had to go in today so they could start putting the estimate together.'

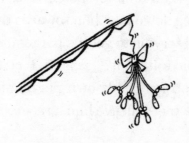

A mean old man decides to treat his wife to the Christmas present of a flight in a light aircraft. Just before the flight, however, he gets into a terrible row with his wife over the price, because he thinks £100 per person is too expensive. In the end, just to shut the pair of them up, the pilot tells them that he will take both of them up together for £100, but on the strict condition that there is no more arguing.

'If I hear a word from either of you while we're up in the air,' says the pilot, 'you'll have to pay the extra £100.'

The couple agree and get into the plane. The pilot takes them up in the air and, feeling a bit sorry for them at this stage, decides to give them the ride of their lives. He makes the plane twist and turn and does a couple of loop the loops.

Incredibly, the old couple don't say a thing, despite all these exciting aerial acrobatics. When they get back down on the ground, the pilot says, 'I can't believe that. I did all the most exciting tricks I know up there but still I didn't hear a peep out of either of you.'

'Well,' says the old man, 'I was going to say something when my wife fell out of the plane during the first loop the loop, but £100 is £100.'

For his Christmas present Mark's wife pays for him to have the tattoo he's been talking about all year. She takes him to the tattoo shop and tells them he wants a huge picture of an Indian across his back. The tattooist starts work.

After thirty minutes, Mark tells his wife, 'Don't forget to get him to do a great big tomahawk in one of his hands.'

'He'll do that in a minute,' says his wife, 'He's just finishing the turban at the moment.'

Geoff's wife has always wanted to keep tropical fish, so he decides to go and buy her some for her Christmas present.

He goes to a pet shop and the owner asks him, 'Do you want an aquarium?'

'I'm not bothered,' says Geoff. 'I don't care what star sign they are.'

George's wife tells him that she's got him a very exciting present for Christmas: she's going to take him for an evening at a lap dancing club. The man protests that he's not really interested in that sort of thing, but his wife insists on taking him along for his special treat. At the entrance to the club, however, George's wife is surprised when the manager appears and seems to know her husband already.

'Happy Christmas, George!' says the manager. 'How are you?'

'How does that man know who you are?' asks George's wife.

'It's because he went to the same school as me,' says George.

Inside the club, a cloakroom girl says, 'Happy Christmas, George. How are you tonight?'

George hastily explains to his wife that he knows the cloakroom girl because she is the girlfriend of one of his work colleagues.

When George and his wife sit down a waitress comes over and says, 'Happy Christmas, George. Do you want your usual?'

George tells his wife that she used to be the barmaid in the local pub.

Finally, one of the dancers passes by and

says, 'Happy Christmas, George! Just wait there and I'll come over and do a special performance for you.'

By this point, George's wife has had enough. 'This was meant to be a special Christmas treat for you,' she says, as she drags him outside, 'but clearly you have been coming here for years. I want to go home now. I have never been so humiliated in all my life!'

The club doorman calls them a taxi, which turns up a minute later.

The taxi driver winds his window down and says, 'Oh boy, George! You've picked up an ugly one tonight.'

Harry's wife gets him a novelty present for Christmas. It's a gadget that tells both your weight and your fortune. Harry tries it out straight away.

'Look at that!' he says. 'It says I'm very intelligent, attractive and an amazing lover.'

'Bloody hell!' says his wife. 'I bet it's got your weight wrong as well.'

TIME TO GET IN THE SPIRIT

Which is your favourite drink to enjoy at
Christmas?
a) *hot, spicy wine*
b) *warm, spicy wine*
c) *cold, spicy wine?*
That is a mulled tipple choice question.

A drunk comes out of a hotel where a big
Christmas party is being held. He manages to
crawl to a taxi waiting at the stand outside and
tells the driver:

'I say, cabbie! Take me to the Connaught
Hotel please!'

'You're there already, you drunken fool,' says
the driver.

'Oh good,' says the drunk man. 'Thanks very
much. Just one thing – next time, don't drive
quite so fast!'

A newspaper article about a festive break
at a luxury hotel once promised:
'Their three-night Christmas break
includes a packed programme of family
entertainment, a crèche, excellent cuisine,
and a visit from Satan.'

A couple are entertaining some friends with Christmas drinks.

The husband tells his wife, 'That lemon we had must have been past its use-by date. When I picked it up it felt all furry.'

'You idiot,' says his wife. 'You've just squeezed my canary into somebody's drink.'

A man is at a big Christmas party in a bar. He goes to order a drink and asks how much the beer is.

'Four pounds a pint,' says the barman, 'or ten pounds for a pitcher.'

'Nah. I think I'll just have the pint,' says the man. 'I don't want my photo taken at the moment.'

A man arrives home drunk after an evening at the office Christmas party. His wife is waiting for him at the door and when she sees him, she is furious.

'Look at the state of you!' she snarls. 'It's perfectly obvious what you've been up to. You've been canoodling with one of the women you work with.'

'No, I haven't,' protests the man.

'Oh yeah?' says his wife. 'Then how do you explain that lipstick there on your collar?'

'That's incredible!' says the man. 'I have no explanation for that at all. I thought I'd taken the bloody thing off!'

A policewoman is out on Christmas Eve checking for drunk drivers when she sees a vehicle swerving all over the road. She stops the car and goes to speak to the driver. The driver falls out of the car and walks unsteadily towards the officer.

'What's the matter?' he asks.

'Well, look at you,' says the policewoman. 'You're staggering.'

'Thanks very much, love!' says the man. 'You're not too bad looking yourself!'

In the run-up to Christmas, Barry goes out for a few drinks with his mates from work. By the end of the evening, he realizes he's had quite a few and so will be well over the limit.

'There's nothing for it,' says one of his friends. 'You'll just have to leave your car here and get a bus home instead.'

The next day his friend asks him how he managed on the bus.

'It was fine,' says Barry. 'Even though it was quite late, I managed to find a bus and it got me home safely and without problem. So, I was quite surprised.'

'Why was that?' asks his friend.

'Well,' says Barry, 'I'd never driven one before.'

A priest is driving in his car on Christmas Eve when he is stopped by the police. The policeman smells alcohol on the priest's breath and notices an empty wine bottle on the floor of the car.

'So, father, tell me truthfully,' says the policeman, 'have you been drinking?'

'No, officer,' says the priest. 'I'd only ever take water when I was driving.'

'OK,' says the policeman. 'Then why can I smell wine?"

The priest looks down at the bottle on the floor then throws his gaze up to heaven and exclaims, 'Praise the Lord! He's done it again!'

A reindeer walks into a bar and orders a pint of lager. The barman pours the reindeer his lager and puts it on the bar for him. The reindeer produces a £10 note. The barman takes the note and gives the reindeer a couple of pounds' change from the till.

'To be honest,' says the barman as he hands over the change, 'we've never had a reindeer come in this bar before.'

'Yeah,' says the reindeer. 'And at these prices, I'm not flipping surprised!'

It's Christmas Eve and a traffic cop has to pull over a car for speeding. The policeman walks over to the car and is about to take the driver's details but then pauses and tells the driver: 'Listen, It's Christmas Eve and I need to end my shift in five minutes. I want to go home and not have to sit doing my paperwork back at the station. So, if you can give me an excuse I've never heard before, I'll let you off this time. So ... tell me why you sped past me just now.'

The driver thinks then says, 'It's like this, officer. Ten years ago, my wife left me for a policeman and when I saw you in my rear-view mirror, I became concerned that that man was you ... and you were bringing her back to me.'

Late on Christmas Eve, after the pubs have closed, a drunk wanders up to a policeman and says, 'Excuse me, officer. But could you tell me what the time is?'

Hearing this the policeman gives the drunk a bop on the head with his truncheon and says, 'One o'clock.'

'Ow!' squeals the drunk. 'I'm glad I didn't ask an hour ago.'

Every Christmas a man visits a bar and orders three pints of beer. He then sits on his own and drinks each of the beers, one after the other. After a few years of seeing him do this every Christmas, the barman tells him: 'You know, you don't have to order your drinks all at once.'

'I know,' says the man, 'but I have two brothers. One moved to the USA. The other moved to Australia. We don't ever see each other anymore, so we vowed that every Christmas we would have a drink together. Each of my brothers is sitting somewhere out there on the other side of the world, each of them in another bar and each of them with three beers in front of him. That way we can all share a Christmas drink together.'

The barman thinks this is a very nice tradition, but then a few years later, Christmas comes around again and he sees the man order only two pints of beer.

'Oh, I'm so sorry,' says the barman. 'I presume this must mean that one of your brothers has died?'

'No, not at all,' says the man. 'They're both still perfectly fine. It's me: this year I gave up drinking.'

It's Christmas in the pub and Dave goes up to the bar and asks the barman if he could have a double.

'OK,' says the barman and disappears round the back, only to appear again a few moments later with another man who looks exactly the same as Dave.

Ron has been enjoying a few Christmas drinks. He picks up a can of beer and, printed on the side, reads: 'Best drunk before 2023'.

He then spends the rest of the evening phoning his mates to tell them that he thinks he's just won an award.

The landlord of a pub decides to set a challenge for his patrons on Christmas Eve. He pours twenty pints of beer, lines them up on the bar and tells his customers he is offering a Christmas bet. If anyone can drink all of the pints, one after the other, not only will he get the drinks for free he will also win £100.

One man puts his hand up and says he will have a go but he just needs to go somewhere first. He leaves the pub, then comes back thirty minutes later and proceeds to down the twenty pints, one after another.

The landlord is impressed and hands him the cash.

'There's just one thing,' says the landlord. 'Where did you go to for that half an hour?'

'Ah, well,' says the man. 'Before I took your bet I thought I'd better pop to the pub next door and have a go at doing it there first!'

HOME FOR THE HOLIDAYS

Everyone is driving home for Christmas, when a traffic report comes on the radio saying that a lorry carrying a consignment of Vicks Nasal Spray has shed its load on the road ahead of them.

Luckily this should make everyone's journey much easier as police say this should provide no congestion for up to eight hours.

The Definition of Christmas

The time when you can travel back home and cherish the time spent with your family, while at the same time reminding yourself exactly why you decided to move as far away from them as possible.

A man is driving home for Christmas on a long, straight road. He notices a traffic camera and just as he passes it, he sees it flash. He checks his speedometer and sees that he hadn't been exceeding the speed limit. So, he stops, turns round, drives back up the road and goes past the traffic camera again at a slower speed.

Again, though, the camera flashes as he passes. The man is incensed and goes back yet again ... but again he sets off the camera.

In the end he drives past it ten times and each time the camera flashes.

Finally, he goes home to enjoy Christmas and, first thing in the New Year, he receives ten fixed-penalty notices for driving without wearing his seatbelt.

Wilfred grew up in a very poor family. Each year for their Christmas dinner all they had to eat was leftovers. And even worse, they were leftovers from the previous year's Christmas dinner.

A man is driving home for Christmas when he has a terrible collision with a lorry from the local furniture store and is left buried under a pile of hundreds of pillows, duvets and cushions. The local hospital make a statement to say his condition is currently 'comfortable'.

Everyone is trying to get home on Christmas Eve when a woman accidentally crashes into a man's car. Both cars are write-offs but neither the man nor the woman is injured.

They crawl from the wreckage and the woman says, 'Wow! Our cars are completely smashed up but there's not a scratch on either of us. It's a Christmas miracle! In the spirit of the season, we should show goodwill to one another from this day forward!'

'I agree,' says the man. 'It's a sign from God! we should live in peace for the rest of our lives.'

'And here's another miracle,' says the woman. 'Even though my car is completely wrecked, the seventy-five-year-old bottle of malt whisky I had next to me on the seat hasn't smashed. That surely means that God wishes for us to drink to celebrate the Christmas season together and share this vintage delicacy.'

She hands the bottle to the man who thanks her, opens it and drinks half the bottle before handing it back. The woman takes the bottle back and replaces the cap.

'Aren't you having any?' asks the man.

'No,' says the woman. 'I think I'll just wait until after the police have been.'

A man is booked on a train to go home for Christmas. When he gets in, he tells his wife, 'They gave me a seat with my back to the engine, so I was facing backwards to the way train was going. I hate that!'

'Well then,' says his wife, 'You should have asked the person in the opposite seat to swap with you.'

'No, I couldn't do that,' says the man. 'There wasn't anyone in the seat opposite me.'

A man has booked a flight to go back home for the Christmas holidays. He gets on the plane and finds himself sitting waiting to take off for over an hour. Eventually he calls the stewardess to ask if there is a reason for the delay.

'I'm very sorry, sir,' says the stewardess. 'But our pilot is a little worried about a noise he can hear the engine making.'

'I see,' says the man. 'So we're just waiting for an engineer to come and check the problem?'

'No,' says the stewardess. 'We're waiting for another pilot whose hearing isn't as good.'

Two business travellers are flying back home to be with their families for the Christmas holiday but in the middle of his flight the pilot comes on the tannoy to make an announcement:

'Ladies and gentlemen, I'm very sorry to have to inform you that one of our engines has just failed. There is, however, no reason to worry because this plane can continue to fly with just the three other engines which are all in full working order. Unfortunately, though, the slight loss of power does mean that our two-hour flight will now take three hours.'

The passengers grumble slightly but settle back down again for the rest of the flight until a few minutes later there is another announcement from the pilot:

'Ladies and gentlemen, I'm very sorry to inform you that another of our engines has now failed. Again, there is no reason to worry as the plane can continue to fly with the two remaining engines. It does however mean that the flight will now take five rather than three hours.'

There is more tutting from the passengers but once again they settle down, until a few minutes later there is yet *another* announcement from the pilot:

'Well, I'm terribly sorry, ladies and gentlemen, but we've just lost another one. There is still no need to worry. We can still fly with our one remaining engine but the flight will now take eight hours.'

At this point one of the business travellers turns to the other and says:

'I can't believe this. If we lose any more engines we're going to be stuck up here all night!'

On the last train home on Christmas Eve an inspector comes down the carriage checking everyone's tickets. A drunk man checks his pockets but begins to panic when he can't find his ticket.

'Don't worry,' says the inspector. 'It's Christmas so I'm prepared to let you off!'

'Never mind that,' says the drunk. 'If I can't find my ticket, how am I supposed to know where I'm going?'

A train full of commuters are on their way home on Christmas Eve when the conductor announces over the intercom that one of the engines has broken down.

'But,' says the conductor, 'we should try to look on the bright side. We'll be able to continue our journey because we've still got our secondary engine in full working order.'

Five minutes later the conductor is back on the intercom again to say:

'I'm afraid, ladies and gentlemen, that our secondary engine has just packed in as well. That means we have no power at all and have come to a complete halt. But we should still try to look on the bright side. At least we're not on a plane at the moment.'

Christmas can be a very emotional time. People travel for miles to be with others who they only see once a year. And then they discover once a year is a bit too often.

On Christmas Eve Brian sends a text to his wife to tell her, 'I won't be home till late. Please make sure there's a nice hot meal ready for me when I get in.'

A few minutes later, Brian decides to send her another text: 'By the way, I should have said, I was given a massive end of year bonus today and I've used it to buy you a new car for your Christmas present.'

His wife instantly replies, 'That's wonderful. Thank you so much!'

Tom texts back, 'Nah! Only kidding! I just wanted to make sure you had received my first message!'

IT'S A CRACKER!

How do you know if Father Christmas has got
into your house?
You can sense his presents!

How do you scare a snowman?
By threatening him with a hairdryer!

Where do pirates go to do their Christmas
shopping?
Aaaaaaaaaarrrrrrrrgos!

What you call a man who's scared of Christmas?
Noel Coward.

What did the frog say when he was given a new book for Christmas?
Redit ... Redit ... Redit ...

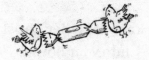

When does New Year come before Christmas?
Every year!

What comes at the end of Christmas Day?
The letter Y!

What's the perfect Christmas gift for the person who has everything?
Medical insurance.

What's red and white and keeps falling down the chimney?
Santa Klutz!

What's red, white and green?
Santa Claus when he's travel sick!

How does Father Christmas keep
his hands clean?
He uses hand Santatizer.

How does a snowman build a house?
Igloos it together.

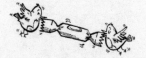

How do you know when you've had a snowman
in your bed?
When you wake up in the morning you're wet.

Why did Santa have to give up smoking his
pipe?
It was bad for his elf.

What do you call a blind reindeer?

No idea.

What do you call a dead blind reindeer?

Still no idea.

Why couldn't Santa find the Christmas cake?
It was stollen.

How did Scrooge win the football game?
The ghost of Christmas passed!

How do you make an idiot laugh on Boxing Day?
Tell him a joke on Christmas Eve!

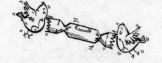

What is a New Year's resolution?
Something that goes in one year and out the other.

What did the cat say on New Year's Eve?
Meow.

What do a Christmas tree and a priest have in common?

Their balls are just for decoration.

How many presents can Santa fit into an empty sack?

Just the one. After that, it's not empty!

How many reindeer does it take to change a light bulb?

Eight! One to screw in the light bulb and seven to hold Rudolph down!

What do you call Santa's cat?

Santa Claws!

What do you call Santa's dog?
Santa Paws!

Who delivers presents to baby sharks at Christmas?
Santa Jaws!

Why do birds fly south in the winter?
Because they can't afford the train!

What did the reindeer say to the elf?
Absolutely nothing. Reindeer can't talk!

What do you call a man who claps at Christmas?
Santapplause!

What do you call someone who refuses to believe in Santa?

A rebel without a Claus!

What do you get if you cross mistletoe with a duck?

A Christmas quacker.

What do you get if you cross Santa Claus with Scarlett Johansson?

A thank you from Santa!

What's the best Christmas present for the person who has everything?

A burglar alarm.

What's the perfect Christmas gift for the
person who has everything?
Something to put it in.

Did you hear about when Father Christmas
tried speed dating?
He managed to pull a cracker!

Knock, knock!
Who's there?
Ho Ho.
Ho Ho who?
I'm afraid your Father Christmas impression
may need a bit of work!

Knock, knock!
Who's there?
Interrupting Santa.
Inter...
Ho ho ho! Merry Christmas!

CHRISTMAS IN HOSPITAL

The local television station is doing a special broadcast from the hospital on Christmas Day. The presenter approaches a man who has been in hospital since a road accident a few days before. The man is now completely covered in plaster and has both his legs hoisted up.

'How are you feeling?' asks the presenter.

'I'm OK but it's very difficult here in hospital,' says the man, and then suddenly leans over on his left, at which point a doctor appears, grabs him and settles him upright in the bed again.

'I can see you're quite uncomfortable,' says the presenter.

'You can say that again,' says the patient, and then suddenly leans over on his right, at which point a nurse appears, grabs him and settles him back upright in bed again.

'So how do you feel about the staff here?' asks the presenter.

'They're OK,' says the man, 'but as you can see, none of them will let me fart!'

A man falls ill and is rushed to hospital for an operation on Christmas Eve. As he is being prepared for surgery, he asks the doctor: 'Is there any chance I'll be back home in time for Christmas?'

'I'm sorry,' says the doctor. 'But if all goes well, you should be out of here in time for New Year.'

'OK,' says the man. 'But what about if things don't go well?'

'Well, in that case,' says the doctor, 'it will be much quicker.'

A woman tells a friend that her husband had to be rushed to hospital on Christmas Day.

'They rushed him in,' says the wife, 'and they only just managed to operate on him in time.'

'How terrible,' says the friend.

'I know,' says the wife. 'Apparently, if we'd left it until after Boxing Day he would have got better all on his own.'

George gets upset during a game of Scrabble on Christmas Day and ends up swallowing a load of the tiles.

He's rushed to hospital where the doctors tell his wife, 'I'm very sorry but this is an extremely serious situation. Your husband's next bowel movement could spell disaster.'

It's Christmas morning and the local TV station is doing a special programme visiting patients in the hospital. The presenter walks through the men's ward wishing everyone Happy Christmas and asks a man in one of the beds what condition he is suffering from.

'Piles,' says the man.

'Oh no!' says the presenter. 'And what treatment are they using to deal with that?'

'A wire brush and some paraffin,' says the man.

'Oh dear,' says the presenter. 'Never mind. Tell me, what are you wishing for this Christmas?'

'I'd like to see all my lovely family come and see me here at visiting time,' says the man.

'Very good,' says the presenter as he moves on to the next patient in the next bed and asks what he is suffering from.

'Piles,' says the next patient.

'Oh no!' says the presenter. 'And what are they using to treat this condition in your case?'

'A wire brush and some paraffin,' says the patient.

'Oh dear,' says the presenter. 'Never mind. Tell me, what is it you are wishing for this Christmas?'

'To have all my family and my grandchildren come to see me at visiting time,' says the patient.

The presenter moves on to the man in the next bed and asks again, 'So what are you suffering from?'

'Laryngitis,' says the third patient.

'Oh no!' says the presenter. "And what are they using to treat your condition?'

'A wire brush and some paraffin,' says the third patient.

'Oh dear,' says the presenter. 'Never mind. Tell me, what is your wish for Christmas Day?'

'To get the wire brush before those other two bastards,' says the third patient.

A patient is in hospital over Christmas. On Boxing Day the doctor comes and tells him, 'We've had your test results back. Which do you want first? The bad news or the very bad news?'

'Oh dear,' says the patient. 'OK. Tell me the bad news first.'

'I'm afraid,' says the doctor, 'that you only have twenty-four hours to live.'

'Oh no,' says the patient. 'So what's the *really* bad news?'

'I should have told you yesterday,' says the doctor, 'but I was off for Christmas.'

Two men are talking in the pub at Christmas. One tells the other, 'I've just had some terrible news. My girlfriend has been involved in a crash and she's lost both her legs.'

'Sorry, mate. That's really terrible for her,' says his friend.

'Never mind that. What about me?' says the first man. 'I bought her a pair of trousers for Christmas and now it's too late to get a refund!'

A man walks into a doctor's surgery on Christmas Eve and asks for an immediate appointment. The receptionist is hesitant to let him in as the doctor was just about to go home. As it's Christmas, however, the doctor thinks there should be good will to all men and agrees to see him.

The man walks into the doctor's room and wanders around for a few moments.

'How can I help you?' asks the doctor.

'Well,' says the man. 'The problem is I keep thinking I'm a moth.'

'A moth?' says the doctor.

'Yes,' the man replies. 'I've become convinced that I'm a moth.'

'I'm sorry,' says the doctor. 'But I'm not sure I can help you. I think you actually need to see a psychiatrist.'

'Yes!' says the man. 'That's exactly what I thought.'

'OK,' says the doctor, 'but if you knew you needed a psychiatrist rather than a GP, why did you come in here?'

'Well,' says the man, 'the door was open and the light was on ...'

Ted and Ernie are talking in the pub after Christmas, when Ted notices Ernie has got a horrible scar across his head.

'What happened to you?' asks Ted.

'It was terrible,' says Ernie. 'I had to go into hospital to have eighteen stitches taken out.'

'Oh no! That's terrible,' says Ted. 'By the way, that reminds me. What did you get for your wife for her Christmas present?'

'A sewing kit,' says Ernie.

It's Christmas and a young couple go into hospital to have their first child. The midwife tells them some disturbing news. The little boy is healthy but all he has is a head: no arms, legs, body or anything. The parents don't mind, however, and take their little boy home and each year give him the most wonderful Christmas they can. But then one year, as Christmas comes around yet again, they are contacted by a famous surgeon who tells them that after years of work he has perfected an amazing new transplant technique. It is now at last possible to cure their child by grafting an entire body onto his head. The parents rush home to tell their little boy the good news.

'Guess what?' says dad. 'This Christmas you're going to get the greatest present you could ever hope to have!'

'It's true, son,' says mum. 'This year we are going to give you the best present you could ever possibly have.'

'Yeah, yeah,' says the boy, rolling his eyes. 'You say that, but I bet it's going to be another flipping hat, isn't it?!'

A middle-aged woman is taken to hospital on Christmas Day after having a heart attack. She nearly dies and while she's on the operating table, she sees a vision of God and prays:

'Oh, Lord, please don't let this be it!'

'OK, my child,' says God. 'As it is Christmas, I will let you have another forty years of life.'

The woman recovers and decides that from this day forward she will make more of her life. So, she stays in hospital to have a facelift, liposuction, a tummy tuck, a boob job and also has her hair dyed. Finally, she leaves the hospital after the last operation and is immediately run down by a bus and dies.

She arrives in front of God and says: 'I thought you told me I could have another forty years?'

'Oh, sorry about that,' says God. 'I didn't recognize you!'

THE LAST DAY AT WORK

A man walks into his boss's office at work and says, 'Sir, as it's coming up to Christmas, I was wondering if you'd consider giving me a rise – especially as I've currently got three other companies who are interested in talking to me in the New Year.'

The boss feels he has no choice but to grant the wage increase rather than lose him.

Just as the man is leaving, his boss asks, 'By the way, which three companies were after you?'

'Oh,' says the man. 'It's my mortgage provider, my internet provider and my credit card company.'

Just before the Christmas break the owner of a big company gathers all his employees together and tells them: 'Thanks to all of you this has been a very successful year for the company. This year I've seen big increases and as a reward, I'm going to give every one of you a personal cheque for £5,000!'

The employees are all very excited by this and begin queuing up, ready for their cheques.

'And then if we do just as well next year,' the owner adds quickly, 'I'll think about signing them.'

A man is involved in a traffic accident while going home from his office Christmas party. He sends a text from his hospital bed to tell his wife: 'Darling, I've just been in a horrible car crash. Georgia managed to get me to the hospital but the doctors have examined me and say that I've got ten broken bones and may need an urgent organ transplant.'

Two minutes later, his wife texts back to ask: 'Who the hell is Georgia?!'

A man is finally ready to leave the office late on Christmas Eve but just as he's going his new boss calls him over.

The boss is standing looking confused, with a piece of paper in his hand in front of the office shredder.

'Before you go,' he says. 'I've got this very sensitive and important document I need to deal with. My PA has already left the office and I'm not sure how this machine works. Can you show me, please?'

'Certainly,' says the man and turns on the shredder, inserts the paper and presses the start button.

'That's excellent,' says the boss, as his paper disappears inside the machine. 'Now if you could just get it to do me one copy …'

SIGNS YOU MAY NOT BE GETTING A CHRISTMAS BONUS THIS YEAR

Your boss has been locked in his office looking increasingly desperate for several weeks.

Just before Christmas your desk is moved to a dark room in the cellar.

You notice your picture has been removed from the staff page on your company's website.

Your colleagues refer to you as the ghost of unemployment future.

Your boss gives you a Christmas card with your P45 inside.

Inside your Christmas card from your boss you find a bill for all the stuff you've been stealing from the stationery cupboard.

You see your boss leaving his office for
Christmas via the window.

*Your Christmas card from your boss comes from
an undisclosed address in South America.*

You are given a Christmas present of a
cardboard box to put all the things from your
desk into.

*As they leave for Christmas your colleagues all
say 'see you next year' to everyone except you (to
whom they just say 'see you').*

You see a picture of your boss on TV together
with an announcement of a reward from
the police for anyone who may know of his
whereabouts.

*You see your boss is in his office having an
earnest discussion with several police officers
while frequently pointing in your direction.*

THANK GOD WE DON'T HAVE TO SEE THEM THE REST OF THE YEAR

Auntie Nora comes to stay for Christmas with her nephew, Clive, and his family.

Clive welcomes her to the house saying: 'You must treat this place as if it were your own!'

'OK,' says Vera. And so, later on, while he's out, she sells it.

'Santa Claus has the right idea – visit people only once a year.'

VICTOR BORGE

Gordon's mother-in-law came round unexpectedly on Christmas afternoon. Gordon says that next year he's going to buy some more effective chloroform.

A man spends all Christmas Day arguing with his mother-in-law, who has come to visit.

'You know what the problem is,' says his wife. 'Whenever she's here you just keep pushing her buttons.'

'I wish I *was* doing that,' says her husband. 'I might have found the bloody mute by now.'

It's Christmas Day in Tom and Vera's house when the phone suddenly starts ringing. Vera answers and starts chatting away. After a while, Tom checks the time and realizes she's been talking for over twenty minutes. A little later, he checks again and by now Vera has been talking for over forty minutes. Finally, after an entire hour, she puts the phone down.

'Sixty minutes!' says Tom, before adding sarcastically. 'That's a short conversation for you!'

'I know,' says Vera. 'It was a wrong number.'

It's Christmas Day and a family sit down to their traditional – and very tense – dinner together.

Afterwards, out in the kitchen, the wife is shaking with rage.

She tells her husband, 'I can't bear this. Why do we have to have that miserable, complaining old woman over for dinner every Christmas? She's never happy with anything we do for her.

From the moment she arrives in the morning to when you take her home again, she does nothing but moan and criticize and boss me around all day. I'm sorry but I've had enough. I don't want your mother coming to us for Christmas ever again.'

'What do you mean "my mother"?' asks her husband, peering out at the old crone sitting at the dining room table. 'I've always presumed she was *your* mother!'

A woman says to her husband, 'Is it all right if my mother comes down for Christmas Day?'

'Oh no!' says her husband. 'Does she have to?'

'Yes, she does!' says the woman. 'She's been up on our roof for almost a week now.'

Sid and Janet have their extended family round for a Christmas party every year. One year, however, some of the guests are a bit disappointed by the spread of food laid on.

One relative asks: 'What happened to that lovely flaky pastry you used to use for your vol au vents?'

'Oh yes. Sorry about that,' says Sid. 'But my dermatitis finally cleared up this year.'

All the family gather for a Christmas party. A little girl is told to say hello to her very elderly great grandmother but she doesn't say a word.

'Come on,' says her mum. 'You must have something to say to someone who has lived for such an amazingly long time?'

'OK,' says the girl, turning back to her great grandmother. 'How come your skin doesn't fit your face?'

In the middle of Christmas afternoon, Trevor hears a knock at the front door. He goes to answer and finds a plumber standing on the doorstep.

'Mr Harris?' says the plumber. 'I've come about your leaking tap in the kitchen.'

'I'm sorry,' says Trevor. 'But Mr Harris moved out of this house over a year ago.'

'I can't believe it,' says the plumber. 'They tell you it's an emergency and then just bugger off before you get there!'

Old Mabel has suffered from deafness for many years. Finally, just before she goes to visit her family for Christmas, she buys herself a small, virtually invisible, hearing aid.

After Christmas, a friend asks her how she got on with the new hearing aid and what her family made of it.

'Oh, I didn't tell them,' says Mabel. 'But it was very interesting being able to hear them talk to each other when they thought I couldn't hear. I've changed my will half a dozen times since Boxing Day!'

Frank tells his mother-in-law to come into the other room for her Christmas present this year because he's got her a special antique novelty chair. But then his wife walks in and catches him just as he's about to plug it in for her.

It's the middle of the night on Christmas Eve and a man is lying in bed when he hears his phone ringing downstairs. He gets up, puts on his slippers and trudges downstairs to answer the phone.

At the other end of the line he hears a voice ask, 'Hello? Is that Santa?'

'No, it's not,' says the man.

'Oh dear,' says the voice on the phone, 'I'm sorry to have bothered you.'

'That's OK,' says the man. 'I had to get up to answer the phone anyway.'

The reason everyone is willing to invite their relatives over for dinner on Christmas Day is because people tend to speak less when their mouths are stuffed with food.

WINTER WEATHER

A severe weather warning is announced on the television news. The conditions outside are very cold and icy, the newsreader says, 'if anyone has to go out they must remember to take a shovel and a blanket, a sleeping bag and plenty of warm extra clothing, as well as food and drink, a can of de-icer, a torch, spare batteries, a first-aid kit and a pair of jump leads.'

Geoff is listening to this and thinks he'd better follow the instructions carefully. Half-an-hour later, he's sitting on the bus wondering why everyone is staring at him.

It's the middle of winter and there has been a heavy fall of snow overnight. A man is walking along the road when he sees a small boy in front of a house frantically shovelling a great pile of snow that lies across the driveway.

'Are you all right?' asks the man. 'Shouldn't you stop for a rest?'

'No, I can't stop,' says the boy.

'But,' says the man, 'that's an awfully big pile of snow for a little boy like you to have to shovel.'

'I've got to do it,' says the boy, 'because my dad told me to shift it.'

'But shouldn't you at least stop to have a drink?' says the man.

'No,' says the boy, 'I can't stop. If I stop for a moment my dad gets really cross with me.'

'Well,' says the man, 'I must say, your dad sounds like a bit of a slave driver to me. I think I should have a word with him. Where is he?'

'He's under this pile of snow!' says the boy.

Because of the winter weather Toby is very careful to follow all the official safety advice when he leaves his house at Christmas. He sets out into the dark winter night having made sure he is dressed from head to toe in brilliant white clothing to make sure he is clearly visible to all motorists.

Unfortunately, five minutes later, he was run over by a man driving a snow plough.

A couple go out for a walk in the middle of December. While they're out the heavens open and it starts pouring down on them. The man has brought an umbrella and puts it up. The umbrella, however, is a wreck with broken prongs and its material all torn.

'You idiot,' says the wife, 'why did you bring that piece of rubbish with you?'

'Well,' says the husband, 'I didn't think it was going to rain.'

It's a freezing cold day in the run up to Christmas and a wife sends her husband a text saying: 'Windows frozen'.

The husband sends a message straight back saying: 'OK, to unfreeze them what you need to do is get a jug of warm water and pour it over them. Let me know if that does the trick.'

Five minutes later he gets another text back saying: 'Didn't work. Computer is completely buggered now.'

A Scottish man phones the emergency services on Christmas morning to tell them that he has just seen a yellow, glowing UFO floating above his house.

'I think you'll find,' the operator tells him, 'that that is, in fact, the sun.'

An Englishman calls a friend in Outer Mongolia.

'How can you bear to live in such cold conditions?' asks the Englishman.

'What do you mean?' says his Mongolian friend. 'It's not too bad here.'

'But I just saw on the news,' says the Englishman, 'that it's minus seventy where you are.'

'No,' says the Mongolian, 'it's fine. It's only about minus thirty really. So, it's not too bad at all. I think they must be lying to you on your TV news.'

'Wow!' says the Englishman. 'That still sounds really cold. And they showed massive snowdrifts and everyone going round in big fur coats.'

'Oh, I see,' says the Mongolian, 'you're talking about *outside*!'

It's Christmas night and the famous Viking warrior Rudolph the Red is at home with his family. His young son looks out of the window and says, 'It's snowing!'

'No,' says dad, 'that's just rain.'

'It's snow!' says the boy.

'Don't argue with your father,' says his mum. 'Rudolph the Red knows rain, dear.'

> **The best thing about a heavy downpour of snow is that it makes your garden look just as good as anyone else's.**

One day in December Bert got knocked off his bike by the salt spreading truck. As he picked himself up, he yelled after the truck through gritted teeth.

Dave and Vera live in a very snowy area. During the middle of December an announcer comes on the local radio and says: 'We are going to have around six inches of snow today, so the local council has issued the following order. All residents must park their cars on the even numbered side of their street in order to allow the snowplough to get through and clear the road.'

At this Dave gets up and goes out and to move his car.

A week later there is another announcement on the radio: 'This week we are going to have at least eight inches of snow, so the council has issued the following order. All residents must park their cars on the odd numbered side of their street to allow the snowplough to get through and clear the road.'

Again, Dave goes straight out to move his car.

The following week there is yet another announcement on the radio: 'This week we are going to have around over twelve inches of snow, so the local council has issued the following order ...'

But just at that moment the power cuts out

and they don't hear the rest of the instructions. Dave is very concerned.

'This is terrible,' he says. 'Now I've got no idea which side of the road to park the car to let the snowplough through.'

'OK, here's an idea,' says Vera. 'Why don't you just leave it in the garage this time?'

One of the great mysteries of life is why at Christmas, when it's cold, do we all turn our central heating up to make our houses the same temperature as they were during the summer, when we were all complaining that it was far too hot.

Following storm damage earlier in December, Bert has a visit on Christmas Day from a trio of arborists.

'Who is it?' calls his wife.

'I can't believe it!' calls Bert. 'It's the tree wise men!'

A man goes to Germany for the Christmas holiday and takes his dog with him. While he's there he goes out ice skating on a frozen lake but as soon as he steps on the ice, his dog dashes past him in excitement, cracks the ice and falls through into the water.

Luckily, a local man is there and he dives in after the dog, pulls him to safety and proceeds to start giving the animal the kiss of life.

'Are you a vet?' asks the man.

'A-vet? Are you kidding?' says the German. 'I'm a-bloody soaking!'

It has been snowing all through Christmas week and Chas's mother-in-law has spent her time just looking sadly through the window.

'You know, I feel a bit sorry for her,' says his wife.

'You're right,' says Chas. 'I'll tell you what. If the weather gets any worse, I think we'd better let her in.'

On Boxing Day two idiots are found outside a cinema frozen to death in the snow. They had been queuing up to see: *Closed for Christmas Due to Bad Weather.*

NO TIME LIKE THE PRESENTS

It's late on Christmas night and Tom has forgotten to get any presents for his family. On the way home from the pub, however, he manages to pick up a bunch of flowers for his wife and some cuddly toys for the kids … Living round the corner from an accident blackspot turns out to have unexpected advantages.

Among his Christmas presents a man receives two scarves, one blue and the other red, from his mother.

On Boxing Day he goes over to see her and decides to wear the blue scarf. She opens the door and before anything else says: 'What's the matter? You didn't like the red scarf?'

> **As all dads know, if it weren't for Christmas as well as Father's Day and birthdays, there would probably be no reason for aftershave to exist.**

At Christmas an angel appears to a man and tells him, 'Because you have done such good works and been so virtuous over the past year, I can offer you a choice of three Christmas gifts. When you wake up on Christmas morning, I can make you either the most handsome man in the entire world; or I can make you the wisest man in the entire world; or I can make you the wealthiest man in the entire world.'

The man thinks for a moment before deciding he would like the gift of wisdom.

'Your wish will be done,' says the angel.

And sure enough, the man wakes up on Christmas morning as the wisest man in the world and immediately thinks, 'Damn it! I should have taken the money.'

'I was going to exchange my brother one time after Christmas, but my mom would never tell me where he came from.'
MELANIE WHITE

Just after Christmas, two men are talking. 'Did your wife like the present you got her?' asks one.

'No,' says the other. 'She hated it. She had asked me to get her something in silk. But I think in the end I must have got her the wrong colour emulsion.'

Kevin's mum and dad buy him a car for his Christmas present.

'It's only had one careful owner,' says dad. Kevin goes out to look at the vehicle and finds that it's covered in bumps and scratches.

'I thought you said it had only had one careful owner,' says Kevin.

'It has,' says dad. 'The rest of them were all maniacs.'

Ronnie is always losing all the remote controls he has for his TV, DVD player and satellite box. For Christmas his wife buys him the perfect present, a brand-new remote control that will work with all the different pieces of equipment.

'Brilliant!' says Ronnie. 'This will change everything!'

Len gets a new laptop for Christmas but then has trouble setting it up.

'What's wrong?' asks his wife.

'I can't understand it,' he says. 'I've put in exactly the password it shows on the diagram in the instruction book but it still won't work.'

'Oh yeah? What password was that?' asks his wife.

'Asterisk, asterisk, asterisk, asterisk, asterisk, asterisk!' says Len.

Ollie gets a new computer for Christmas. The computer asks him to create a password, so he types in 'incorrect'.

Now if ever he forgets his password and types in something else by mistake, his new computer will specifically tell him: 'Your password is incorrect'.

Phyllis got her husband Pete an *Aloe vera* plant for Christmas. He was very pleased with it but unfortunately, a few minutes later, he accidentally sat on it.

This caused a very unpleasant and painful injury to his backside ... but luckily it healed very quickly.

On Christmas Day Bob opens his present from his wife. 'Just what I needed!' says Bob. 'Some new underwear!'

'Well,' says his wife. 'They're new to you!'

On Christmas Day a man presents his wife with a beautifully wrapped little gift.

She takes off the paper saying, 'Is this what I think it's going to be?'

'Yes,' says her husband. 'I did just what you asked and got you something with diamonds on it.'

A moment later her face drops as she discovers that he's bought her a packet of playing cards.

On Christmas morning Fred's wife asks him, 'So where's my Christmas present?'

Fred has to improvise quickly and a brainwave comes to him. 'This year,' he says, '*I'm* going to be your present!'

'Bloody hell!' says his wife. 'I hope you kept the receipt.'

Old Albert is taken to the shops by his daughter, who wants to buy him a new hearing aid for Christmas. The shopkeeper first brings out a tiny hearing aid no bigger than a pea.

Unfortunately, it is far too expensive, so Albert's daughter asks if the shopkeeper has anything cheaper.

He goes away and next brings out a hearing aid about the size of a small battery. Again, it is very impressive but it also extremely expensive.

So, once again, Albert's daughter asks if there is anything cheaper available. The shopkeeper pulls out another hearing aid, this time the size of a wallet which could fit in a pocket and connect to an earpiece via a thin wire.

Unfortunately, even this model is too expensive for Albert's daughter, who asks yet again if there is anything a little cheaper.

By this stage, the shopkeeper is getting a little frustrated but nevertheless he goes away and returns with another model of hearing aid.

This one comprises a brass horn, about three feet across, which connects to a box about the size of a biscuit tin, which, in turn, connects to the ears via a pair of large black headphones.

'This is the cheapest we've got,' says the shopkeeper.

'OK, so how does it work?' asks Albert's daughter.

'It doesn't,' says the shopkeeper. 'But at least when people see the old man with it they'll begin to speak louder.'

Eddie receives a copy of the *Pirates of the Caribbean* DVD for Christmas.

He notices that on the box there is a printed warning about piracy and says to his wife:

'I would have thought the clue was in the title.'

Sid tells his friend Tony: 'For Christmas this year, I've bought my wife a new wooden leg.'

'That's nice,' says Tony. 'Is that for her main present?'

'Of course not,' says Sid. 'It's just a stocking filler.'

Two men are showing each other their Christmas presents.

'I got this crystal ball,' says one, 'but it only seems to predict terrible weather.'

'To be honest,' says his friend, 'I think you might have just got a snow globe.'

Lance and Ron are two horrible old male chauvinists.

'What did you get the wife for her Christmas present?' asks Lance.

'I got her a belt and a bag,' says Ron.

'That's very kind of you,' says Lance. 'I think you might be spoiling her.'

'I know,' says Ron. 'But hopefully the vacuum cleaner will work better now.'

Two men are talking after Christmas. One tells the other, 'My wife hit the roof when she opened her Christmas present.'

'Really?' says his friend.

'Yes,' says the first. 'I suppose I should have warned her I'd got her a self-inflating dinghy.'

For his Christmas present Trevor has asked for subscriptions to two magazines: *National Geographic* and *Playboy*.

'I don't know why you want either of those,' says his wife. 'They're both full of pictures of places you won't be visiting any time soon.'

A woman gets her husband a new shirt for Christmas. As he unwraps it, she explains that it's a very expensive shirt made from a brand-new unique and completely unshrinkable fabric that is guaranteed to keep its shape no matter what you do to it. He tries it on but it's too big.

'Don't worry,' says the woman. 'It'll shrink in the wash.'

It's Christmas morning in a house in the middle of Liverpool and a family of scousers are opening their presents. The daughter of the family tears the wrapping paper off one present and discovers a book.

'There's the book you asked for, love,' says her mum. 'You'll be able to learn to speak to people from India now you've got this *Introduction to Urdu!*'

'No! This isn't what I asked for at all!' says the daughter. 'I wanted a book on how to be a hairdresser!'

Bert's family are opening their presents on Christmas morning. He finds a large package under the Christmas tree and carries it over to his mother-in-law.

'Oh! What's this?' she asks.

'Well,' says Bert, 'you know you've been saying you'll need to burn off some calories after Christmas?'

'So, you've got me some exercise equipment?' asks his mother-in-law.

'No,' says Bert. 'I got you a flamethrower.'

Old Stan hasn't been too good on his feet for years and has had to go round bent double and walking with the aid of a stick. But then a few days after Christmas, a friend sees him out walking and now standing straight up.

'That's amazing!' says his friend. 'Have you had some sort of miracle cure?'

'No,' says Stan. 'My family got me a longer stick for Christmas.'

A family are exchanging their Christmas presents. Auntie Mabel is known for being very frugal in her gift purchases.

'It's the thought that counts, not the gift,' she tells her little niece as she opens her present and looks disappointed.

'I know, auntie,' says the little girl, 'but could you maybe try thinking a bit bigger?'

In early January a man strides angrily into an antiques store, complaining about the statue he bought there for his wife's Christmas present.

'When I bought this statue, you told me it was made from the finest ivory,' complains the man.

'Yes, that's true,' says the antiques dealer, 'I can assure you that the material definitely came from an elephant.'

'Really?!' scoffs the man. 'In that case, when they shot it, the elephant must have been wearing dentures!'

A man asks for some Viagra for his Christmas present. His wife gets him a pack and prepares for some excitement but is then surprised to see him crumbling the tablets into his tea.

'What are you doing?' she asks.

'Oh,' replies the man, 'I just wanted it to stop my biscuits going soft when I dunk them.'

A man asks his wife what he can get her for Christmas and she tells him she would like an expensive jar of wrinkle cream.

'Why do you want that?' asks the man. 'I thought yours were all natural.'

A man buys his elderly mother a fancy new Teasmade for Christmas. On Christmas Day, the man takes her her present, sets it up next to her bed and explains how it works. A few days later he calls her up and asks how she likes her present.

'It's wonderful!' she says. 'But there's one thing I don't understand. Why do I have to go to bed every time I want a cup of tea?'

A man tells a friend: 'I got a really cheap dictionary off my mum for Christmas and now I just can't find the words to thank her.'

A man tells his friend he bought his wife a new non-stick frying pan for her Christmas present.

'Is it any good?' asks the friend.

'We don't know yet,' says the man, 'we're still trying to get the sticky label off before we can use it.'

A man tells his friend the only Christmas gift he got from his wife was a pack of cards, which all seemed to have something sticky over them.

'Oh dear,' says the friend. 'That doesn't seem a very nice present.'

'No,' says the man. 'To be honest I find it very hard to deal with.'

A woman asks her friend: 'Are we exchanging presents this Christmas?'

'Well,' says the friend, 'I certainly always have to exchange yours.'

A student gets back to college after Christmas.

'How was it?' asks her friend.

'It was an absolute disaster,' says the student. 'I told my mum and dad what I wanted for Christmas was some money so I could buy myself a new laptop.'

'OK, so what happened?' asks her friend.

'The worst possible thing,' says the student. 'They just bought me a new laptop!'

A very old doddery gentleman walks into a West End jewellers with a beautiful young woman. He tells her to go and choose whatever she would like for her Christmas present. She spends a while looking around, before choosing a very expensive diamond necklace.

'Will you accept a cheque?' asks the old man.

'Of course, sir,' says the sales assistant. 'But I'm afraid we will have to wait a few days for your cheque to clear. Once it has done so, you can come back to take delivery?'

'No problem,' says the old man, and he and the young woman walk out arm in arm.

The day after Boxing Day the man returns, this time alone, to find the sales assistant is furious with him.

'I don't know how you can dare to show your face in here again,' says the sales assistant. 'It turned out your cheque bounced because there was no money in your bank account whatsoever.'

'Yes, sorry about that,' says the old man. 'I just came back to apologize for your trouble – and also to thank you for the greatest Christmas I've ever had!"

Madge buys her friend Sue a gold locket for Christmas.

'What do you think you'll put in it?' asks Madge.

'A lock of my husband's hair,' says Sue. 'It will be a lovely reminder of happier times.'

'But your husband's still alive,' says Madge.

'I know,' says Sue, 'but he's going bald quite quickly now.'

A woman goes into a chemist's and says, 'I want to get my husband a nice deodorant for Christmas.'

'OK,' says the chemist. 'Do you want "ball" or "aerosol"?'

'Neither,' says the woman. 'It's for under his armpits.'

Back in the 1980s Ted received a CD of the new Dire Straits album for his Christmas present.

CDs had only just appeared on the market and Ted had heard you could spread jam, peanut butter and gravel on them and they would still play perfectly. And unfortunately he discovered this to be completely true ...

Christmas arrives and a man has forgotten to get his wife any presents. So, he comes up with a cunning plan. On Christmas morning, he presents her with what he calls her first gift. She takes the paper off and inside finds a stick that has a star made from aluminium foil stuck on one end.

'What the hell is this meant to be?' asks his wife.

'I've got you a magic wand,' says her husband. 'If you wave it and say the magic word – "Abracadabra!" – then something magical will happen.'

Eventually his wife is persuaded to do as he says. She takes, the wand, waves it from side to side and says, 'Abracadabra'.

'Oh no!' says the man. 'I'm afraid you did it wrong – and now you've made all your other presents disappear!'

Barry's wife isn't impressed by the presents he gets her for Christmas.

'If you get me any more stupid gifts this year,' she tells him, 'I'm just going to burn them.'

So he buys her a candle.

Nigel's wife tells him that she is going to buy him the thing he has always wanted for his Christmas present.

'Really?!' exclaims Nigel. 'An antique gold watch! Wait a minute! It's not a wind up, is it?'

Beryl tells her friend, 'My boyfriend gave me a surprise present for Christmas this year.'

'That's nice,' says her friend.

'Not really,' says Beryl. 'I'm on antibiotics for it now.'

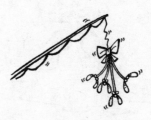

Clarrie gets her husband a nice new deodorant for Christmas and he takes it into the bathroom to try it out. A minute later she hears him cry out in sudden pain and when she opens the door, she finds him in a state of some discomfort, having misunderstood the instructions on the label, which say to 'remove from wrapper and push up bottom'. Afterwards, he walks rather awkwardly but on the plus side, every time he farts the room smells of ylang ylang.

Gus's dad was a millionaire. He had made his money walking round the streets on Christmas morning, just after all the children had opened their presents, yelling: 'Batteries for sale!'

Ged receives a framed painting of the Leaning Tower of Pisa for one of his Christmas presents. By the middle of January, he's still trying to find a way to hang it so it looks right.

Frank gets a call from his elderly dad after Christmas. Frank's dad wants to check how his grandson enjoyed Christmas.

'Oh, he loved it,' says Frank. 'But unfortunately, he's broken all his presents.'

'Oh no!' says granddad.

'Yes,' says Frank. 'The new PlayStation we got him is all smashed. His new phone is smashed too. And his new iPad.'

'What about the present I got him?' asks granddad.

'Don't worry about that,' says Frank. 'Your hammer is absolutely fine.'

Granddad is given a state-of-the-art digital camera for his Christmas present. He spends the rest of the day taking photos of the family opening all their presents and enjoying their Christmas together but unfortunately he isn't quite on board with new technology and ends up with thirty-six pictures of his own eye.

Harry is a model railway fanatic, so for Christmas his wife gets him a massive new train set, which he lays out all round the attic.

A few days later his friend Tom calls round and finds Harry outside in the garden in the rain having a cigarette.

'Why aren't you inside enjoying your new train set?' asks Tom.

'I can't at the moment,' says Harry. 'All the trains are non-smoking.'

It's Christmas morning and a family are moaning to one another about the presents they get each year from their penny-pinching old auntie.

'I can't believe she just gets us the same thing every year,' says the son.

'And she just goes down to the local supermarket and spends no more than a pound on each of us,' says the daughter.

'Now, now,' says mum, 'stop moaning, the pair of you. It's very good of her to get you anything.'

'We know,' say the kids, 'but what are we going to do with yet *another* pair of shopping trolleys?'

It's Christmas afternoon and Eddie is wandering round the house looking for something.

'What's the matter?' asks his son.

'I need a newspaper,' says Eddie. 'It's terrible that there aren't any available on Christmas Day.'

'You don't need a newspaper these days,' says his son. 'Here! Just have a go on the new iPad you got for Christmas instead. It will give you everything you want from a newspaper and more!'

'That's great, son,' says Eddie.

And with that he takes the iPad and walks off with it into the next room. A sound of crashing and smashing then follows, before Eddie comes back with the iPad now shattered into pieces.

'Thanks, son,' says Eddie. 'That bluebottle never knew what hit it.'

When Tom was a child he used to pray every night that he would get a new bike for Christmas. Eventually he realized that God didn't work that way. So he stole a bike and prayed to God for forgiveness instead.

Billy's mum and dad always thought he was a strange child. Every year when Christmas came around they would ask him what he wanted for his main present and year after year he asked for exactly the same thing: a pink golf ball. They tried offering him all sorts of other exciting presents but Billy was insistent that all he wanted was a pink golf ball.

And so, for every Christmas throughout his childhood, all Billy's mum and dad were ever able to buy him was pink golf balls.

But then when he was sixteen his mum said, 'This is stupid. We can't keep buying him pink golf balls. Surely he's got to be interested in something else by now.'

So that year his parents decided instead to buy him a shiny new bike. On Christmas morning, Billy woke up and found his bike – and thankfully he really liked it. After breakfast he decided to go out for a ride and went into the town centre, where he saw the local sports shop with a pile of pink golf balls in the window. He turned right across the road to go and have a closer look but was immediately knocked off his bike by a passing car.

Billy's mum and dad rushed to the hospital

to see him. The doctor told them that tragically Billy wasn't going to make it and probably didn't have long left. They went to his bedside, where dad couldn't help himself from asking one last question before his son passed away.

'Billy,' he whispered. 'There's just one thing I want to know. You've never played golf in your life, you've never been interested in watching golf on television, so why on earth have you only ever asked for pink golf balls for Christmas?'

Billy turned to his parents. He smiled and opened his mouth to speak but before a sound came out, he suddenly died.

So, the moral of the story is, 'Don't forget to wear your helmet when you go out on your bike.'

A family decide to bring their old granny into the computer age and buy her her very own laptop for Christmas. They then have to teach her how to use it. They show her how to open Google and tell her how useful it is for looking up any information she wants to know, but she still protests that she doesn't know how it works.

'Look, gran,' says her grandson. 'It's very simple. All you have to do is type in a question you want to know the answer to, just as though you were writing a letter asking a friend something.'

'OK,' says gran. 'I'll give it a go.'

And then she proceeds to type into Google: 'Hello, Mavis. How are your haemorrhoids getting on at the moment?'

DINNER WITH ALL THE TRIMMINGS

A family invite all their relatives over and sit down together for Christmas dinner.

After they've finished eating, the mum of the family says, 'Well, I have to admit that I was a bit worried about making dinner for all of you but in the end it seemed to go well.'

'Yes,' says her little daughter, 'I told you they'd never notice the turkey was four months past its sell-by date.'

Scientists have managed to cross a turkey with a zebra to create the world's first four-legged Christmas dinner that comes with its own barcode.

On Christmas Eve, Simon forgets to close the fridge door properly before he goes to bed. The next morning, he and his wife come downstairs and discover that all the food they have for Christmas has gone off overnight.

His wife is furious and yells at him, 'You idiot! What am I going to do with all this food now?'

'All right! Calm down!' says Simon. 'There's no need to make a meal out of it.'

On Christmas Day dad makes the dinner for the family. They sit down to eat but aren't impressed at all with the meal he has prepared.

'Ugh!' says one of the children. 'This is just like eating horse manure.'

'Now, don't be rude,' says mum. 'That's not true at all! Horse manure is usually warm ...'

Christmas Day ended up causing a terrible mess in Fred Astaire and Ginger Rogers' house. They got dressed up in their finest outfits but ended up throwing the Christmas dinner all over each other.

'Oh no! Just look at me!' said Fred 'I've got pudding on my top hat, pudding on my white tie, pudding on my tails ...'

In the middle of the night after Christmas, a woman wakes up her husband and tells him, 'I've just been downstairs and someone's broken into the house and gone into our kitchen and started eating the remains of the Christmas dinner I made for us.'

'Oh no,' says the husband, and reaches over for his phone and rings the emergency services.

'Are you calling for the police?' asks his wife.

'No,' he says. 'An ambulance.'

Tom tells Stan that every Christmas Day he has pigs in blankets.

'For your Christmas dinner?' asks Stan.

'No,' says Tom. 'It's what I call the in-laws when they come and sleep in our spare room.'

A man has been sent to the shops to get the food for Christmas dinner. He goes into a greengrocer's and asks for three pounds of sprouts.

'Sorry, mate,' says the greengrocer. 'We only sell kilos these days.'

'Do you?' says the man. 'OK, in that case I'll have three pounds of kilos instead.'

A man is doing the big newspaper Christmas crossword. He calls to his wife for help.

'What's the answer to this one?' he yells. '"A flightless bird from Iceland".'

'That's easy,' says his wife. 'It's a frozen turkey, isn't it?!'

An old lady goes to her nephew's family for Christmas dinner. As they're waiting to sit down, she asks one of the children if they're having a traditional turkey dinner.

'No,' says the child, 'I think we're having goat.'

'That's odd,' says the old lady. 'Are you sure you've got that right?'

'Oh yes,' says the little girl. 'I heard daddy say that as it was Christmas, we were going to have to have the old goat for dinner.'

A woman is out shopping on Christmas Eve, trying to choose a turkey.

She asks the butcher how much they are and he holds up two birds and says, 'I'll tell you what. Because it's Christmas Eve, I can do you a special offer. You can have these two for £15.'

'Right,' says the woman and points at one of the turkeys. 'But how much would it be if I just bought this one?'

'That would be £10 on its own,' says the butcher.

'OK,' says the woman. 'I'll just have the other one for £5 then.'

A woman walks into a butcher's to buy her Christmas turkey. She chooses a bird and then spends several minutes prodding and poking it. She picks up one wing and sniffs beneath it. Then she lifts the other wing and does the same. Finally, she picks the whole turkey up and peers down its rear end – and gives this a sniff as well. At last, she says, 'This turkey is not fresh!'

'Lady,' says the butcher, 'tell me honestly, do you think *you* could have passed the same test?'

A young couple who have just moved into a flat together decide to make Christmas dinner for themselves for the first time. They get a turkey but then find they have difficulty preparing it. The boy phones his mum to ask for some advice.

'Why?' asks his mum. 'What's the matter with this turkey?'

'Well,' says the boy, 'for a start it won't keep still.'

It's lunchtime on Christmas Day and Terry hears his wife's voice from the kitchen asking: 'What do you want for your Christmas dinner, my love? Turkey or beef?'

'I'll have the turkey thanks, darling,' calls Terry.

'You're having beans on toast,' his wife snaps back. 'I was talking to the cat!'

Harry makes dinner for the family on Christmas Day. After they've finished their main course, he asks them what they would like for their pudding.

'The antidote!' says one of his children.

Two men are going round the supermarket shopping for their Christmas dinner.

One of them tells the other, 'It's quite difficult for me finding things to eat because I'm a vegan.'

'Doesn't that affect your health?' asks the other.

'Only my sight,' says the first. 'Apparently I've damaged my eyes trying to squint at the small print on all the ingredient labels.'

REALLY, IT'S ALL FOR THE CHILDREN

A little boy comes down on Christmas morning.

'Look at all the lovely Christmas presents that Father Christmas has left you,' says his mum.

The little boy finds all his Christmas presents under the Christmas tree, each one with a label signed: 'Happy Christmas! Love from Father Christmas'.

He goes through them all one by one, opening them eagerly and revealing a number of exciting gifts. When he's finished, however, he looks rather sad.

'What's the matter?' asks his mother.

'To be honest,' says the little boy, 'I was really hoping you and daddy might have got me something as well.'

'Nothing's as mean as giving a little child something useful for Christmas.'

KIN HUBBARD

A young girl asks her mum, 'Mummy, where do all my Christmas presents come from?'

'Well,' says mum, 'they come from Father Christmas, of course.'

'Oh,' says the little girl. 'And where do babies come from?'

'They come from the stork,' says mum.

'And who keeps us safe in our house?' asks the little girl.

'Well, that's the police,' says mum.

'And what about if the house was on fire?' asks the little girl.

'Then it would be the firefighters,' says mum.

'And if we're not well, who makes us better?' asks the little girl.

'That would be our doctor,' says mum.

'And where are we getting our Christmas dinner from?' asks the little girl.

'From the supermarket,' says mum.

'Right,' says the little girl. 'So in that case, what *exactly* do we need daddy for?'

A little boy tells his friend at school that last year all he got for Christmas was a lump of coal.

'So, what did you do this year?' asks his friend.

'I decided I'd get even and leave a poisoned mince pie for the bastard,' says the boy.

'Wow! Did it work?' asks the friend.

'No!' says the boy. 'He somehow found out my plan and when I woke up on Christmas morning, he'd killed my dad – using exactly the same poison!'

'Oh no!' says the friend.

'I've learned my lesson now,' says the boy. 'Never mess with Santa!'

A man buys his children a set of batteries for their Christmas present.

He sticks a note on the packet to say: 'Toys not included.'

Frank tells a friend, 'I never got any Christmas presents when I was a kid.'

'That's really sad,' says his friend. 'Didn't you believe in Father Christmas?'

I did,' says Frank. 'The problem was, so did my mum and dad.'

On Christmas Day a little girl comes up to her daddy and asks, 'Daddy, what is "sex"?'

Her dad is shocked but then thinks his daughter is beginning to get a bit older and it's natural for her to start asking questions, and Christmas Day is as good a time as any to explain the facts of life.

So, he sits her down and starts going through a short lecture on all aspects of sexual reproduction, the workings of men and women's sexual organs and the various sexual activities and inclinations that adults can have.

After a few minutes of this he asks her, 'Why did you ask me about this now?'

'Because,' says the little girl, 'mummy just asked me to come and tell you that Christmas dinner will be ready in a couple of secs.'

Gus's kids were driving him mad because they spent all December trying to find where their Christmas presents were hidden. In the end he had no choice but to put them all up in the attic. Now he can't get any sleep because they keep banging on the attic door asking to be let down again.

Halfway through January a man tells his wife: 'Oh no! I just realized we forgot to give our daughter one of her Christmas presents. I can't believe we forgot about that pony. Especially after all that effort hiding it at the back of the closet.'

'Ah!' says his wife. 'I was wondering what that smell was.'

A little boy gets a violin for his Christmas present from his grandfather. A few days later he thanks his granddad and tells him it's the best present he's ever had because he's been making lots of money from it.

'That's wonderful!' says his granddad. 'You must have learned to play very quickly. Are you putting on concerts?'

'No,' says the boy, 'Mum gives me money not to play it in the daytime and dad gives me money not to play it each night.'

After Christmas the little boy continues to practice on his new violin but every time he starts playing a tune, the family's dog lifts its head up and begins howling loudly and sounding as though it is in great pain.

As soon as the little boy stops playing, the dog stops howling but then as soon as he starts the next number, the dog starts up all over again. After twenty minutes or so of teeth-gratingly awful noises from the violin and – even more excruciating noises from the dog – dad has had enough.

He marches in, snatches the violin off the little boy and says, 'For goodness sake! Why can't you find a piece of music that the dog doesn't know!'

As soon as the shops are open after Christmas, dad snatches his son's new violin and takes it to the local antiques shop. He takes the instrument out of its case, shows it to the owner and says, 'This is my son's violin. How much can you give me for it?'

The antiques dealer examines the violin. 'It's a nice instrument,' he says. 'I can offer you £200.'

'Never mind,' says dad. 'I know someone else who is offering twice as much to take it off my hands.'

'Oh yes,' says the shop owner. 'Is it another antiques dealer?'

'No,' says dad, 'it's our next-door neighbour.'

'I gave my young nephew a book for Christmas.
He's spent six months looking for where to put the
batteries.'
MILTON BERLE

A little boy and his mum are doing their Christmas shopping. All the way round the shops the little boy keeps biting his fingernails. His mother keeps telling him to stop or Father Christmas will not come to him this year but still he carries on biting them. Finally, she has had enough.

She sits him down and tells him: 'Look! If you don't stop biting your fingernails, do you know what's going to happen to you? All those dirty bits of fingernail are going to get stuck somewhere deep inside your tummy and nothing will be able to get through and you will then start to get bigger and bigger and bigger until you eventually go pop and burst right open.'

The little boy is horrified but the story does the trick and he stops biting his fingernails. Later, on the bus on the way home, the little boy notices a pregnant woman sit down opposite them. He keeps staring at her large tummy until she asks crossly:

'Excuse me! Do you know me?!'

'No,' says the little boy, 'but I know what you've been doing!'

A primary school class are back after Christmas. Their teacher says that each of them can get up in front of the class and tell everyone about one special present they had received for Christmas.

The first little girl gets up and says: 'This year for Christmas I got a bow-wow!'

'Now,' says the teacher, 'you're not babies any more. You are old enough to know and use the correct names for things. So, I don't want to hear any more baby talk. What is the proper name that a grown up would use for the present you got?'

'A puppy dog,' says the little girl.

'Very good,' says the teacher. 'Who wants to go next?'

Another child gets up and says, 'This year for Christmas I got a choo-choo!'

'No!' says the teacher. 'Tell us again but use the proper grown-up term for what you got.'

'I got an electric train,' says the child.

'That's better,' says the teacher. 'Who else wants to go?'

A little boy gets up and tells the class, 'I got a book.'

'Very good,' says the teacher. 'Tell us a bit more. What was the title of the book you got?'

The boy thinks hard for a moment then says: *'Winnie the Turd!'*

'There's nothing sadder in this world than to awake Christmas morning and not be a child.'

ERMA BOMBECK

A woman takes her young son round the shops just before Christmas. When they get home, she finds his pockets stuffed with chocolate and sweets, and a load of toys and a new games console hidden inside his coat.

'Where did you get all this?' she yells. 'Because I know you didn't buy them and I certainly didn't buy them. So, tell me the truth. Were you stealing things all the way round the shops?'

The boy hangs his head and shamefully admits his guilt.

'Right,' says the woman. 'We're going straight back – and this time we're calling in at the jewellers!'

Mum and dad have ordered a special Christmas present for their children but it comes flat-packed for home assembly.

The package arrives and they read the instructions and begin to assemble the kit. After a few minutes they realize they have been sent the wrong item and write to the company to complain that they had ordered a kit for a treehouse but instead received the materials for a sailboat.

A few days later the company replied saying: 'We apologize that you were sent the incorrect item and regret the inconvenience you have experienced. Nevertheless, please bear in mind this will have been nothing compared to that of another of our customers who is currently out on a lake somewhere trying to sail your treehouse.'

'My parents always said I was a gifted child. Turns out they meant someone left me on their doorstep in a box.'

UNKNOWN

The kids open their presents on Christmas morning but discover that all their new toys need batteries.

'Don't worry,' says dad. 'I picked up a load of batteries for you the other day. You can get as many as you want from the local recycling centre.'

'Didn't you have to pay for them?' ask the kids.

'No,' says dad, 'it said they were all completely free of charge.'

Shortly after Christmas a man is waiting at the traffic lights in his car when a little girl pulls up beside him on a bright pink bike with a basket at the front, stabilizers, reflectors on the wheels and streamers dangling from the handlebars. The little girl knocks on his window and he winds it down.

'This is my new bike,' says the girl. 'I got it for Christmas. Do you like it?'

The man says that he does like it, so the girl says, 'Well, in that case, do you want a race?'

The man chuckles, the traffic lights change, he winds up his window, hits the accelerator and sets off doing nought to sixty in a couple of seconds.

When he looks in his mirror, however, he sees the little girl on her bike coming up behind and shooting past him at extraordinary speed, yelling: 'Heyyyyyy!'

'What the hell?' says the man and shifts into top gear to speed past the girl again. Once again, however, he sees her in the mirror gaining on him and shooting past, still shouting to him while doing over a hundred miles an hour on her little bike, as sparks and smoke stream from her training wheels.

A couple of seconds later he comes to a bend and finds the little girl and her bike in a heap at the side of the road. He stops and goes over to check she's OK.

'What was it you were trying to shout to me as you came up behind?' he asks.

'You got my streamers stuck in your window when you wound it up,' says the little girl.

A little girl is writing a thank-you note to all her aunties and uncles for the Christmas presents they sent her. She is writing the notes extremely quickly, so her dad looks to see what she's writing. Each note turns out to have nothing in it except the entire alphabet from A to Z.

'What's this?' asks dad.

'Well,' says the girl, 'mum said to do all my thank you notes to my aunties and uncles but I don't know what to write to them. So, I just thought I'd put in all the letters of the alphabet, and then they can rearrange them however, they think best.'

A man sees a young boy in the park with a big Christmas selection box full of chocolate bars. The boy sits eating one bar from the box then takes another and scoffs that down and then another and another.

'That's a lot of chocolate you're getting through,' says the man. 'You know, it isn't very good for you. It'll rot your teeth and make you fat and eventually give you all sorts of health problems.'

'Oh really?' says the boy. 'Well, my granddad lived to be a hundred.'

'Oh yes?' says the man. 'But did he spend his time eating entire boxes of chocolate all at once?'

'No,' says the boy. 'Mostly he just minded his own flipping business.'

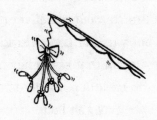

SIGNS THAT SANTA HATES YOUR CHILD

Your child receives their letter to Santa back, now covered in red marks where their spelling and punctuation has been corrected.

Your child receives an official-looking note saying your home is no longer on Santa's delivery route.

On Christmas morning your child discovers their presents have been dropped all the way down your chimney and now lie smashed to pieces in the fireplace in the living room.

On Christmas morning your child finds a note saying that Santa tried to deliver their presents in the night but was unable to do so and it is now necessary for them to instead be picked up from your nearest depot located at the North Pole.

Your child receives their letter to Santa back with the message 'Dream on, kiddo!' scrawled across the page.

On Christmas morning your child wakes to find a note from Santa telling him an excess delivery charge needs to be paid before his presents can be delivered.

On Christmas morning your child wakes to find a note from Santa making a detailed and damning critique of the mince pie and brandy left out the night before.

On Christmas morning your child wakes to find a note from Santa, across which Santa has written in big letters 'I DON'T REALLY EXIST, YOU KNOW!'

Your child discovers their Christmas stocking is completely stuffed with all the packaging from the presents Santa delivered to all the other children.

Your child comes down on Christmas morning to find the living room carpet covered with reindeer poo.

FATHER CHRISTMAS DO NOT TOUCH ME

A small child tells his friend, 'You know Father Christmas works very hard all through the year making toys. So, you have to be very good, or he won't bring you anything for Christmas.'

The friend replies: 'I don't think he works that hard. I saw him in the shopping centre yesterday and he just seemed to be sitting round doing nothing all day.'

Father Christmas goes to see a psychiatrist. The psychiatrist asks him, 'What seems to be the problem?'

'It's terrible, doctor,' says Father Christmas, 'I've stopped believing in myself.'

'I stopped believing in Santa Claus when I was six.
Mother took me to see him in a department store,
and he asked for my autograph.'

SHIRLEY TEMPLE

**Father Christmas is a very jolly fellow!
Imagine having to do all that driving and
still being able to say 'Ho! Ho! Ho!'**

How can you tell Santa Claus is a man?
*No woman would keep wearing the same outfit
again and again every year.*

On Christmas night why does Father Christmas
visit China first?
*He needs to stock up on all the presents for
everyone else.*

A man asks his friend, 'What nationality is
Santa Claus?'
The friend thinks for a moment then says,
'I think he might be North Polish.'

It's Christmas Eve and Santa is preparing to go
on his rounds, delivering presents around the
world. Just before he sets off, however, an official
from the Aviation Authority turns up and tells
him, 'I'm afraid before you take off, I will need to
check your sleigh, to make sure it's airworthy.'

Santa has no choice but to let the official do
all his basic checks. Afterwards, the official tells
Santa, 'That's OK, but now I need to sit in with
you for a test flight.'

The official climbs aboard, Santa cracks his
whip and his reindeers pull the sleigh up into
the sky. Santa is then alarmed to see the official
pull out a gun and aim it at one of the reindeer.

'What's going on?' asks Santa. 'You're not a
hijacker are you?'

'Of course not,' says the official. 'But I do
have to check what happens if you lose one of
your engines shortly after take-off.'

The year you stop believing in Father Christmas tends to be the same year you start being given clothes for Christmas.

On Christmas Eve, a little boy runs to his mother shouting, 'Mummy! Mummy! Come quick! Father Christmas is in the kitchen and he's kissing the au pair girl.'

His mum leaps up looking alarmed, at which point the little boy starts laughing and says:

'Ah, you fell for it! It isn't really Father Christmas at all. It's daddy!'

A little boy is taken to see Father Christmas at the local department store. He waits in the queue and goes into the grotto, where Father Christmas says, 'Ho! Ho! Ho! little boy! So, what would you like for Christmas?'

At this the little boy kicks Santa on the leg and says, 'Why weren't you listening when I told you yesterday!'

A UFO is approaching Earth's atmosphere. Two aliens on board are leading a massive invasion fleet. Suddenly they see something fly past. It's an overweight man with a beard in a flying sleigh pulled by a team of eight hoofed animals with large antennae coming out of their heads, moving at near hyper-speed.

One of the aliens turns to the other and says, 'Actually, I think we better just turn back. The technology on this planet is too advanced.'

The police launch a full-scale investigation into Father Christmas.

They have discovered he wears a beard. He has no discernible source of income but nevertheless manages to come by limitless expensive gifts. And he spends much of his time flying around all the cities and countries of the world, freely entering a variety of different properties.

They're pretty sure he must be involved in the money laundering business.

Terrible news for Santa this year. Rudolph has been hit by a 747 and a flock of seagulls on Christmas Eve while making a gift delivery to Barcelona. But then, as the old saying goes, the reindeer in Spain is hit mainly by the plane.

FESTIVE TRADITIONS

On Christmas night Ted turns to his wife Gladys and tells her, 'I love Christmas! At what other time of the year could we sit in our living room like this, in front of a dead tree, chomping down walnuts out of one of your old socks!'

Angus is a grumpy old man who hates Christmas. He particularly hates it when carol singers come to his door, so to avoid answering, he always turns all his lights off and pretends that he's not in. This wouldn't be quite so bad except for the fact that he works as a lighthouse keeper.

Gordon is going round the town centre doing his Christmas shopping when he sees a brass band playing a selection of carols, with dribble constantly pouring out of the ends of their instruments.

'That's absolutely disgusting,' says Gordon.

'We can't help it,' says one of the musicians. 'We're the Band of the Salivation Army.'

A newspaper carries a story about the lead actor in the local pantomime who had been mugged during the performance. To be fair, the audience had tried to warn him several times.

Two boys are talking at school about their chocolate-filled Advent calendars.

One tells the other, 'This year my mum's got me the official Microsoft advent calendar.'

'Is it any good?' asks the other.

'No. It's rubbish,' says the first, 'I haven't been able to open windows 8 or 10 at all.'

Do you think when she's at home in Buckingham Palace, the Queen likes to refer to her Christmas Broadcast as *The One Show*?

The Christmas charity panto performance for the local paranoid society descended into complete chaos. Someone shouted, 'He's behind you!' and the rest of the audience all went berserk.

Question Master on TV quiz: 'Name a tradition associated with Christmas.' Contestant: 'Hanukkah!'

A special circus comes to town to entertain the kids during the Christmas holidays.

Just before the first show of the day, however, the human cannonball comes to the circus owner and tells him, 'I'm getting a bit old and I've decided I'm going to retire.'

The circus owner gets extremely upset about the late notice, so the human cannonball tells him, 'Don't worry. You'll be able to train someone else up.'

'Never mind that!' says the circus owner. 'Where are we going to find someone of the same calibre?'

In the run-up to Christmas a family go to the big pantomime at the local theatre. Dad has a few drinks before the show and so, by the interval, he realizes he's in desperate need of the toilet. He goes out of the auditorium and asks the usher for directions.

'Go through the doors,' says the usher, 'down the stairs, along the corridor, turn left, turn right, turn left again, you should then see a bright light ahead of you and that's the toilet.'

Dad wanders off slightly confused by all the directions but eventually he finds a brightly lit toilet and spends the next few minutes relieving himself. He finds his way back to his seat some way into the second half of the show.

'Did I miss anything?' he asks.

'Yes,' says mum. 'You missed the best bit of all. While you were away a man came on stage, unzipped his trousers in front of everyone and wee'd into the orchestra pit for five minutes!'

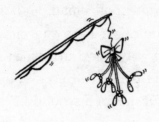

IT MAY BE BEST TO LEAVE YOUR CAR AT HOME

The police get a call late on Christmas Eve from a drunk man.

'Help, police!' says the drunk man. 'I've just got in my car and thieves must have got in because they've taken the dashboard, the steering wheel, the brake pedal, even the accelerator. Oh no. Wait a minute. I've just got in the back seat by mistake.'

On Christmas Eve, a traffic policeman pulls over a car that is being driven erratically. The policeman walks over to the driver and says, 'I believe you've been drinking, sir.'

'Don't be ridiculous!' says the driver. 'I swear to God that I haven't touched a drop all night.'

'OK,' says the policeman. 'Can I see your licence?'

'Very well,' says the driver as he begins fumbling in his pockets. 'Here. Would you just hold my beer for me for a second ...?'

An old couple are driving home after doing their Christmas shopping. Suddenly they hit an icy spot on the road and find themselves sliding downhill fast, unable to stop themselves.

'Oh my God! What are we going to do?' screams the old man, panicking.

'Calm down,' says his wife. 'Brace yourself! And try and crash into something that doesn't cost too much!'

A man walks into a pub in the middle of the countryside. He goes up to the bar and tells the barman: 'Help! I'm lost. I need to go into central London to do my Christmas shopping. Could you tell me the quickest way to get there?'

'Are you walking or driving?' asks the barman.

'Driving,' says the man.

'Ah good,' says the barman. 'Because that's definitely the quickest way.'

A car breaks down in the middle of the Christmas rush. The driver thinks he's going to be lucky to get anyone to come out and fix his car at this time of year, but nevertheless a mechanic turns up.

The mechanic opens the bonnet, checks the engine and then reaches into his tool bag for a hammer. He then proceeds to bash part of the engine with his hammer.

'Try it now,' says the mechanic.

The driver turns his ignition and sure enough the car starts first time.

'OK. That'll be £300!' says the mechanic.

'What do you mean £300?' says the driver. 'All you did was hit it with a hammer. You're just taking advantage because it's Christmas.'

'OK,' says the mechanic. 'I'll write you an itemized bill.'

He then spends a minute writing out a bill, hands it over and the driver reads: 'Hitting engine with hammer – £10. Knowing exactly *where* to hit engine with hammer – £290!'

Gertie gets a lift home in a taxi on Christmas Eve. She becomes concerned when the driver goes over the speed limit and darts from lane to lane among the heavy traffic, barely missing the other cars and almost running three red lights.

'Don't worry!' the driver tells her. 'Just close your eyes and you'll be fine. Trust me: that's what I always do.'

An old man drives off to do his Christmas shopping. After a few minutes his mobile phone rings. He answers and hears his wife's voice: 'Be careful out on the road today. Not only is there heavy traffic but there's just been a newsflash on the radio saying there's some idiot driving the wrong way up the motorway.'

'Tell me about it!' says the old man. 'And it's not just one. There's hundreds of them!'

A traffic officer stops a man for speeding on Christmas Eve.

'Do you know how fast you were going?' asks the policeman.

'I was only trying to keep up with the rest of the traffic,' says the man.

'I can't see any traffic,' says the policeman looking up the road.

'I know,' says the man, 'That's how far behind I am.'

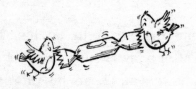

It's the middle of winter and an old lady is out in her car when she sees another vehicle on the road, shedding its load all over the highway. She drives up alongside it, winds down her window and shouts across to the other driver: 'Hey! Did you know there's stuff falling out of the back of your truck? It's going all over the road!'

'Yes, I know it is,' says the driver. 'This is the gritting lorry.'

Two nuns are in a panic trying to get through the busy traffic so they can get to church on time on Christmas Eve.

Another car cuts in front of them and one of the nuns says to the other: 'Maybe that man doesn't realize we're nuns. Sister, you better show him your cross.'

'OK, I will,' says the other, then winds down the window and yells, 'Oi! Get out of the way, you ****ing arsehole!'

WINTER SPORTS

On Boxing Day four married men are out on the course playing golf. The first says, 'You three have no idea what I had to do to get my wife to let me come out for a round of golf over Christmas. I had to promise her that I'd redecorate the house first thing in the New Year.'

'That's nothing,' says the second man. 'I had to promise my wife that I'd get our kitchen re-fitted in January.'

'That's still nothing!' says the third man. 'I had to promise my wife that I'd let her go on a no-expense-spared shopping trip to the January sales.'

A few minutes passed and they realized that the fourth man hadn't said anything, so they asked, 'So, what did you have to do to be allowed out to play golf today?'

'Nothing much,' says the fourth man. 'I just set my alarm for 6.30 a.m. and when it went off, I nudged my wife and said: "So ... golf or sex?" And she said: "Don't forget to wear the jumper I got you for Christmas!"'

Two men go out in a kayak in the middle of winter. Eventually they realize it's freezing, so they light a fire in the boat.

Unfortunately – but unsurprisingly – this causes the vessel to sink, which just goes to prove the old saying: you can't have your kayak and heat it.

Of all the winter sports skiing is the best way to combine outdoor fun with knocking down trees with your face.

It's the middle of winter and a football team are out on a practice session when a huge turkey comes strutting out to join them on the pitch. The players watch in astonishment as the turkey walks up to the team manager and demands to be given a trial.

The turkey proceeds to take possession of the ball time and time again and run right through the defence to score.

When he finally comes off the pitch, the manager says: 'You're actually very good. If you agree to sign with us for the season, I'll make sure you get a huge bonus.'

'I'm not bothered about the bonus,' says the turkey. 'All I want to know is, does the season go past 25 December?'

For her Christmas holiday a woman goes away skiing. She goes up the ski lift to the top of a slope but immediately realizes she desperately needs a pee. There's no toilet anywhere in sight but she spots a small clump of trees, so she goes over to them and drops her ski pants. She breathes a huge sigh as she relieves herself but doesn't realize that she's beginning to slowly slide backwards.

Eventually it dawns on her that she's moving, but by this time it's too late. She's left her ski sticks behind. She begins to pick up speed as she shoots down the slope, still peeing as she goes.

Her bottom begins to turn blue as it gets pelted by the flying snow and her entire ordeal only ends when she crashes backwards into a post.

An hour later, she is admitted to hospital with a broken arm and a bruised blue bottom. In the waiting room, she finds herself sitting next to a man dressed in ski clothing and with his leg in plaster.

'Well,' says the woman. 'It looks like we've both had some bad luck today. How did you break your leg?'

'You'll never believe it,' says the man, 'but I was just going up in the ski lift this morning when I looked down and saw a woman skiing backwards down the mountain with her trousers down round her ankles while having a pee. I leaned over to take a better look and fell straight out of the ski lift. So ... what happened to your arm?'

A team of chess enthusiasts check into a hotel and are standing in the lobby talking in loud voices while discussing all their recent victories. After an hour, the manager comes out and tells them they're all going to have leave.

'Why? What's the matter?' they ask.

'Because,' says the hotel manager, 'if there's one thing I can't stand it's chess nuts boasting in an open foyer.'

The Prime Minister decides to go ice skating on a frozen lake on Christmas Day. Unfortunately, the ice begins to crack and she falls through. Three boys are playing nearby and come to help. They pull her out of the freezing water and the Prime Minister is so pleased she says she will buy each of them a special Christmas present for having saved her.

She asks what they would like. The first asks for a new PlayStation.

'That's fine,' says the Prime Minister. 'I will get you a new PlayStation.'

The second asks for a new football kit.

'That's fine,' says the Prime Minister. 'I will get you a new football kit.'

The third boy, however, asks for a wheelchair.

The Prime Minister is confused. 'Why do you want a wheelchair?' she asks. 'You don't appear to be disabled in any way?'

'I know,' says the boy. 'But I'm still going to need one, once I tell my dad I saved the Prime Minister.'

In the middle of December an idiot decides to go ice fishing. He reads up on the subject, gets all the necessary items together and sets off. He finds a suitable spot on the ice, positions his footstool and then starts to cut a circular hole through the ice.

Suddenly, from somewhere above, a voice boomed out: 'THERE ARE NO FISH UNDER THE ICE!'

The idiot is startled and moves further along and begins to cut another hole.

Again, a voice from above bellows: 'THERE ARE NO FISH UNDER THE ICE!'

The idiot is now a bit concerned and moves as far as he can, to the other end of the ice, before again trying to cut a hole.

Once more the voice thunders out: 'THERE ARE NO FISH UNDER THE ICE!'

The idiot drops to his knees, joins his hands in prayer, looks skywards and says: 'Is that you, oh Lord?'

'No,' replies the voice. 'It's the ice-rink manager!'

At Christmas, Bob and Alf go on a skiing trip but they get caught in a snowstorm and have to pull into a farm. They knock on the door and an attractive woman answers. The woman takes them in out of the storm and lets them sleep on the chairs in her living room. Next morning, they go on their way and enjoy skiing for the rest of the Christmas week.

A few months later, however, Bob receives a letter from the woman's lawyer.

He calls up his friend Alf and says, 'You remember that nice looking woman at the farmhouse who put us up on our skiing holiday? You didn't get up in the middle of the night and go up to her room and have sex with her, did you?'

'Actually, now you mention it, yes, I did,' says Alf.

'I see,' says Bob. 'And when you had sex with her, did you by any chance not tell her your real name?'

'I'm afraid that's also true,' says Alf.

'And did you happen to use my name instead of your own?' asks Bob.

'I'm very sorry about this,' says Alf, shamefaced. 'That is also true. Why do you ask?'

'Well,' says Bob. 'You must have been very good because she's just died and left the entire farm to me.'

Barry's local ice hockey team had a terrible experience. They drowned during spring training.

TIME TO GET FIT AGAIN AFTER CHRISTMAS

What is the longest month of the year?
Dry January.

After Christmas, a man goes to his doctor, who tells him he will have to go on a diet to get his weight back down again.

'What you must do,' says the doctor, 'is have your meals as normal for two days. But then I want you to skip a day. After that eat normally for another two days and then skip another day. Keep doing that for a few weeks and you could lose five pounds.'

A few weeks later, the man is back and has lost four stone.

'That's amazing,' says the doctor. 'Did you follow my instructions?'

'Yes,' says the man, 'and it nearly killed me.'

'From all the dieting?' asks the doctor.

'No,' says the man. 'From all the skipping!'

A man goes to the doctor about all the weight he has put on over Christmas. The doctor tells him he should start an exercise programme but that he should only do this very gradually.

So for the first few weeks of January he starts driving past the gym each day.

Gus puts on a lot of weight over Christmas. By January he's so heavy that one day he falls over and manages to rock himself to sleep while trying to get back up again.

A woman tells a friend that after Christmas she went on a diet and gave up drinking for all of January.

'Did you lose anything?' asks the friend.

'Yes,' says the woman. 'January.'

Percy has piled on so many pounds over Christmas, he thinks he'd better go and ask his doctor what he should do.

The doctor looks him over and says, 'Percy, I don't want to upset you by telling you you're obese. However, if I had to name my five most overweight patients, you'd be at least three of them.'

A woman goes on a diet after Christmas. She tells her friend, 'Look at me! I've lost 2 stone!'

'Are you sure about that?' says her friend. 'If you look in the mirror and turn sideways, I think you might be able to find both of them again.'

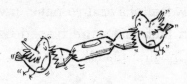

It's an interesting fact that the average woman will burn more calories going round the shops at Christmas for a couple of hours than she would if she spent the same time at the gym.

The reason is that, before Christmas, the average woman will probably be dragging her average husband along behind her.

In January, a woman decides she wants to try and lose weight. To encourage herself to eat less she finds pictures of slim supermodels from a magazine and sticks them up all over the fridge. Over the next month she manages to lose half a stone but unfortunately her husband puts on three quarters.

First thing in January Norma goes to her local gym to sign up for Pilates.

'OK,' says the gym instructor, 'when you come in for the class, make sure you are wearing loose clothing.'

'But I don't have any loose clothing,' says Norma. 'In fact that's the reason I need to do Pilates in the first place.'

A woman weighs herself a few days after Christmas and then calls to her husband, 'Hey, Bert! I'm not sure what calories are but clearly they taste really nice.'

Mary tells a friend that her husband has been on an intensive diet all through January.

'Has he lost much weight?' asks the friend.

'Oh yes,' says Mary. 'He's been losing ten pounds a week so far. Hopefully, if he carries on like this, I'll be rid of him completely by next Christmas.'

Belinda gets an exercise treadmill for Christmas. A few days later a friend asks her how she's getting on with it.

'OK,' she says, 'but so far I've only managed widths.'

A man tells his friend that his doctor has advised him that if he doesn't lose twenty-five per cent of his body weight very soon, he will not make it until next Christmas.

'How did your wife take the news?' asks the friend.

'She was great,' says the man. 'She was so upset she made me a lovely six-course meal to try and cheer me up!'

After Christmas, an overweight man takes up horse riding as an exercise.

And it works! After only a week, the horse lost fifteen pounds!

Alf managed to lose 323 calories on Christmas Day. He was sitting down with a cup of tea and the dog stole his mince pie.

A man asks his doctor what he should do about the excess weight he has put on over Christmas.

'You need to run five miles a day for the next hundred days,' says the doctor.

A hundred days later the doctor calls up the man to see how he's getting on.

'Have you done what I said?' says the doctor.

'Yes, I have,' says the man.

'And have you have lost the weight?' asks the doctor.

'Yes, I have,' says the man.

'That's excellent.' says the doctor. 'Are you able to come into the surgery tomorrow morning for a check-up?'

'Not really,' says the man. 'I'm now five hundred miles from home!'

After Christmas, Harry's doctor tells him he has to start doing some exercise to lose weight. A week later, Harry tells the doctor he's doing ten sit-ups every morning as soon as he wakes up.

'That's good,' says the doctor. 'Are you able to do any more than that?'

'No,' says Harry, 'that's the maximum number of times my alarm clock lets me use the snooze button.'

A man enrols at a health club to try and lose some weight and manages to lose thirty pounds just on the first day.

He got caught on the running machine and had his leg torn off.

After Christmas, Monty goes to a dietician for some advice on how he can begin to reduce his weight again. The dietician looks him over and says, 'OK, the only thing you need to do to lose weight is to move your head from right to left a few times a day.'

'That sounds good,' says Monty. 'When exactly do I need to do this?'

'Any time of day anyone offers you a cake,' says the dietician.

After Christmas, a man decides to start jogging. He sets out from his house but a few minutes later his wife hears him coming back in.

'Did you forget something?' she asks.

'Yes,' he says. 'The fact that if I run for longer than a couple of minutes I'm likely to collapse and die.'

Bob goes to the doctor in January and says he is worried about all the things he ate between Christmas and New Year. The doctor looks him over and tells him, 'To be honest, you should really be more worried about all the things you ate between the New Year and Christmas.'

After the Christmas festivities, Gus starts going to a gym but a few weeks later he tells a friend that he and the gym have had to break up.

'Why's that?' asks the friend.

'Oh, you know,' says Gus, 'things just weren't working out ...'

A man is seeing his doctor because of all the weight he has put on at Christmas. The doctor tells him that to get his true weight he needs to weigh himself completely naked. The man doesn't come back for another six months.

The doctor asks him, 'What happened?'

'I got arrested in the chemists,' says the man.

'I've been on a constant diet for the last two decades. I've lost a total of 789 pounds. By all accounts, I should be hanging from a charm bracelet.'

ERMA BOMBECK

After Christmas, Nigel went on the garlic diet. He didn't lose any weight but his friends all thought he looked thinner because they were standing so far away from him.

A young couple discover that over Christmas the old man in the flat upstairs from them had died. Even worse, when the old man is discovered, the police find that he had drilled holes in his floorboards so he could spy on the young couple below him.

'That disgusting old pervert!' says the woman when she finds out.

'Don't say that. We must remain charitable at Christmas time,' says her boyfriend. 'And even if he was an old pervert, I still like to think he's up there somewhere, looking down on us now.'

Elsie tells her WeightWatchers class that she made her husband a lovely big Christmas cake. He had then eaten half of it after his dinner. She had resisted trying any herself but finally gave in to temptation the next day and cut a small slice.

This was followed by a slightly less small slice, then a larger slice and then a positively huge slice, until the entire other half of the cake was all gone.

She tells the class that she was very upset with her lack of willpower and how disappointed her husband would have been if he had found out.

'How did you stop him finding out?' asks one of the group.

'There was only one way,' says Elsie, 'I made another Christmas cake and ate half of that!'

There is a cure for the common cold consisting of three glasses of whisky. People haven't bothered to develop any different remedies because no one seems interested in them.

In January Bill tells his wife that he's going on a whisky diet.

'How much do you think you'll lose on that?' asks his wife.

'About three days,' says Bill.

'The second day of a diet is always easier than the first. By the second day you're off it.'

JACKIE GLEASON

In January Gerry says he's going on a strict diet. He's not going to eat anything between snacks.

It's New Year and a man who has overdone it over Christmas goes for a medical.

The doctor tells him, 'You're overweight and bordering on the clinically obese.'

'How dare you!' says the man. 'I demand a second opinion!'

'OK,' says the doctor. 'You're an ugly bastard as well!'

It's the middle of winter and Dave picks up a horrible case of the sniffles. He goes to the doctor, who says, 'Yes, this is a horrible bug that's going round. Everyone's got it at the moment. The best thing will be to pump you full of antibiotics to get you over the infection.'

The doctor proceeds to do so and in fact, gives him so many antibiotics, that when Dave sneezes on the bus on his way home, he manages to cure five of the other passengers.

Len goes to the doctor's in January.

The doctor examines him and tells him, 'You're not in good shape and it's entirely because of all the drinking and overeating you did over Christmas.'

'Oh, that's good news,' says Len. 'I thought you were going to tell me it was my fault.'

NEW YEAR

For his New Year's resolution, a man decides to give up smoking, and in order to try and control his cravings he takes up nibbling on wooden toothpicks instead.

Three weeks later, he dies of Dutch Elm Disease.

It's the January sales and a woman goes to a shop with a pile of clothes she had bought just a couple of days earlier, to ask if she can get her money back.

'What was the matter with them?' asks the shop assistant.

'I forgot to take into account all the weight I put on over Christmas,' says the woman.

You should always remember: when the New Year sales begin, try to remain calm and civilized and hold your mobile phone horizontal when recording any fights.

It's New Year's Eve in Trafalgar Square in the middle of London. A drunk falls into one of the fountains and, floundering around in the water, he looks up and sees Nelson standing above him on his column.

'Don't jump!' he shouts in a panic. 'This is the shallow end!'

On New Year's Day a woman surprises her husband by bringing him a lovely tray of breakfast in bed. There is a glass of fruit juice, a bowl of cereal, a plate of bacon and eggs, toast and marmalade and a cafetiere of fresh coffee.

'That looks lovely,' says the husband.

'I know,' says the wife, 'And the reason I'm showing you this is so you'll know how to do it for me for the rest of the year.'

On Christmas Day an elderly couple are looking to the year ahead. 'What will you do,' asks the old man, 'if anything happens to me in the next year and you're left all on your own?'

'Don't worry about that,' says his wife. 'If anything happens to you, I will find a few other women, perhaps a few years younger than me, and I will move in with them and be sitting huddled up with them next Christmas.'

'Yes, you're right,' says the old man, 'I think I'll probably do exactly the same thing.'

Two men are talking at a New Year party.

'What was your New Year's resolution this time last year?' asks one.

'To join the local gym,' says the other.

'OK,' says the first. 'What's your resolution this year then?'

'To start going to it,' says the other.

When the New Year sales begin, always remember to wake up especially early. It's the best way to log on to the internet and see all the fights breaking out.

Colin has worked his way up from humble beginnings to get a nicely paid job. As a result, his family are now always worried about what they would do if anything ever happened to him.

So, on New Year's Day, he tells them, 'You don't have to worry any more this year because I've just taken out very extensive life insurance cover. If anything happens to me, you will receive an amazing monthly income that will pay for you to live in the lap of luxury.'

'Oh dear,' says his eldest child. 'Now I'm worried about what we'll do if you stay alive.'

NEW YEAR'S RESOLUTIONS YOU MIGHT ACTUALLY BE ABLE TO KEEP

Exercise a lot less.

Eat much more.

Waste more time.

Be less careful with money.

Drink so much that the entire year will pass by in a complete blur.

Perfect the art of procrastination.

Take up no new hobbies.

Become less organized.

Spend as little time with friends, family and loved ones as humanly possible.

Maintain a steady rate of physical decline.

Learn something interesting every day and then immediately forget it.

Always remember to live life to the fullest – especially if you can get someone else to clear up after you.